Kids Confidence

A Life-Changing Guide to Boost Your Child's Confidence - Includes The 25 Most Effective Self-Esteem Activities You Can Do Right Now

Scarlett Steele

©Copyright 2022 - Scarlett Steele - All rights reserved

The content within this book may not be reproduced, duplicated, or transmitted without direct written permission from the author or the publisher.

Under no circumstances will any blame or legal responsibility be held against the publisher, or author, for any damages, reparation, or monetary loss due to the information contained within this book, either directly or indirectly.

Legal Notice

This book is copyright protected. This book is only for personal use. You cannot amend, distribute, sell, use, quote, or paraphrase any part, or the content within this book, without the consent of the author-publisher.

Disclaimer Notice

Please note that the information contained within this document is for educational and entertainment purposes only. All effort has been executed to present accurate, up-to-date, and reliable, complete information. No warranties of any kind are declared or implied. Readers acknowledge that the author is not engaging in the rendering of legal, financial, medical, or professional advice.

Table of Contents

Introduction 5

Chapter 1 Into the Child's Mind 9

Chapter 2 Why are Children Insecure? 16

Chapter 3 A Child Who Gives up too Easily 20

Chapter 4 What Negativity Does to Your Child? 27

Chapter 5 How Children's Confidence Changes with Age 33

Chapter 6 Factors that Affect Self-Confidence 45

Chapter 7 The Real Power of Self-Confidence 47

Chapter 8 The Power of the Parent 50

Chapter 9 How to Understand your Child Has Low Self-Esteem When 56

Chapter 10 How Do You Actually Build a Better Relationship with Your Child? 62

Chapter 11 Typical Parenting Mistakes that Affect Children's Self-Esteem ... 65

Chapter 12 Your Contribution to Your Child's Confidence 71

Chapter 13 Recognize Your Success and Fears 74

Chapter 14 Unconditional Love 77

Chapter 15 How to Look Confident 85

Chapter 16 How to Speak Confidently 89

Chapter 17 Self-Esteem Vs Self-Confidence 93

Chapter 18 Self-Esteem 98

Chapter 19 Building Self-Esteem in your Child 105

Chapter 20 Praising Your Child and Self-esteem 118

Chapter 21 Practical Steps to Building Self-Esteem in Children ... 127

Chapter 22 How We Influence Our Child's Self-Esteem 131

Chapter 23 How to Build Resilience in Children 150

Chapter 24 Always Encourage them to Do their Very Best in All Situations 161

Chapter 25 Learn to Accept Your Child for Who He or She is 166

Chapter 26 How to Teach Your Kids to be Strong Mentally and Emotionally Balanced Kids 171

Chapter 27 Exercises for Making Friends 174

Chapter 28 Psychology Tricks to Build Resilience and Unstoppable Confidence in Children 199

Chapter 29 Life Skills to Start Teaching Your Child at Very Early Age for Fortune 208

Chapter 30 10 Ways to Foster Self-esteem and Help a Child Develop a Growth Mindset 219

Chapter 31 The 25 Most Effective Self-Esteem Activities You Can Do Right Now 229

Chapter 32 A Self-esteem-Building Activity Between a Mother and her Daughter 234

Chapter 33 Other Activities that will Help Develop Confidence and Self-Esteem 237

Chapter 34 How to Help Children in Developing Mindfulness to be Prepared for Life 243

Chapter 35 Tools Needed for Children to Develop their Self-Esteem 249

Conclusion 257

INTRODUCTION

Almost all people will become parents at some time in their lives, accounting for around 89.6 percent of the world's adult population. The insurmountable problems of parenthood may leave us befuddled and disillusioned, despite the fact that the majority of us strive to be wonderful parents. As both parents of toddlers and teens will confirm, issues may be seen at any stage of growth in the child's life. But there is some good news: parents now have access to a variety of research-based tools and techniques. This is a welcome development. Various products address typical parenting challenges (such as nighttime troubles, finicky eating, tantrums, behavior problems, and risk-taking) as well as life lessons (starting school, being respectful, making friends, being responsible, making good choices, etc.).

A number of factors combine to aid in the development of children's resilience. They serve as a safety net , helping them develop self-confidence as they grow older. Despite the fact that some of these traits may aid in the establishment of stability, children have a higher chance of developing resilience when all characteristics are present.

A child's network of caring and supportive interactions is essential for resiliency. It may involve parents, teachers, sports coaches, family, and friends. It's critical that the support system include a trustworthy adult, either within or outside the family, someone who can reassure and encourage him to persevere, and recognize the qualities that will help him overcome obstacles.

Building resilience necessitates developing a realistic plan and taking actionable measures to carry it out. A solid plan will clearly define the task (for example, I have a speech to give in class next week), the child's strengths (I like the topic I did well the last time I gave a lesson), and any challenges (for example, I have a speech to give to the class next week, but I get nervous speaking in front of others). An adult can assist the youngster in recognizing the different talents or skills they can employ ("You know how to take five deep breaths to calm down before giving a speech so practice in front of a mirror"). When a child learns how to plan well, they can apply it to making new friends, completing a complex video game level, dealing with bullies, or studying for examinations.

The degree to which a youngster believes in their talents and abilities also plays a role in resilience development. The child may try to avoid the scenario totally if they lack confidence. Examples of avoidance is pretending to be unwell in order to miss an exam or forgetting to bring an assignment to school. Pointing out moments when your child did take a risk and succeeded is a simple method to help them gain confidence. Another technique for boosting confidence is to reduce how great a problem appears to be while supporting a strategy for tackling it in phases. Communication and problem-solving abilities are also vital. It's tempting to assume that resilient kids don't need help, but knowing when and how to get it is a big part of what makes them resilient. Adults will respond more positively to children who clearly articulate their plans and ideas.

Finally, the ability to handle powerful emotions and urges requires solid self-regulation skills. When playing board games or missing a goal in soccer, a youngster may grasp the importance of avoiding anger, but they may lack the emotional skills to manage their disappointments at the moment. Teaching emotion regulation is much easier when the youngster is calm and not in a stressful setting. We can then urge the child to apply the new skill after they have learned it. Turn-taking is an excellent early self-regulation skill since it encourages children to share and curbs their desire, for example, to take a toy from another child.

Self-esteem, or a person's self-worth, is critical for success. It is likely for youngsters to excel in school and accomplish personal objectives if they are confident and comfortable in their skin. As they grow older, they learn to deal with problems and resist peer pressure effectively. Having a good self-image is especially crucial since it helps a youngster feel joyful and capable of establishing intimate connections.

Building children's self-esteem is a continuous process in the home. Allowing youngsters to do tasks independently enables them to develop the necessary abilities. When parents show respect, children learn to show respect back. Additionally, when parents express affection, children learn to communicate their feelings to others.

Parents should provide their children with the skills needed to solve difficulties. The ability to deal with challenging circumstances independently will develop as they grow in years. Parenting style dramatically influences a child's character. Nurturing parents who demonstrate their affection contribute to their children's feeling of self-worth. Children learn to be confident and show concern for others. When parents work to raise their children's self-esteem, they lay the groundwork for a long-lasting, loving connection.

The activities of parents have an impact on the way children see themselves. Children sense the importance of their parents when they are held in their arms. Even when parents cannot spend time with their children daily, they still can communicate by phone calls, writing notes, or sending e-mails. When parents talk with their children, they should listen to what they say and show them that their opinions are valued.

Children rely on their parents' unconditional love and support to survive and thrive. As is often believed, parents' love should not be conditional on their children's behavior. At the same time that parents set boundaries and enforce discipline with their children, they should reassure them of their love. When children are denied affection because they have misbehaved, they will begin to feel horrible about themselves. Occasionally, parents may tell their misbehaving kid, "You're a naughty boy (or girl)!" Not the conduct itself, but the child's actions convey the message that they are wrong. The youngster should be told why what they have done is wrong, followed by explaining the consequences. Consider the following scenario: if a youngster hits another, explain that striking hurts and remove the child from the room.

It is beneficial to both parents and children to praise their children when they behave well since this makes them feel good and encourages them to continue the good behavior. Parents should recognize and applaud their children's efforts and accomplishments. After their team loses a game, for example, a parent might tell their child that they tried so hard. "You should be pleased with your achievements!"

Some individuals are concerned that lavishing excessive praise on children could lead to their spoiling. In addition to increasing self-esteem, children also get a more incredible feeling of responsibility and competence. Children feel more valued when assigned duties and receive praise for their achievements. Self-confidence and independence grow, and their growing sense of security provides the ability to cope with the many challenges that are a natural part of growing up, such as peer pressure and bullying.

CHAPTER 1
INTO THE CHILD'S MIND

A child's brain is an amazing thing. It is like a whole universe, just waiting to be explored and discovered. Did you know, until the last decade, scientists and researchers believed that children were just miniature versions of adults? They, for the longest time believed that their minds functioned in the same manner as that of an adult, and it is only a matter of time that they learn new skills and practice them. But since this belief doesn't hold true, we see children depicting behaviors we wouldn't observe in an adult. Things like crying over something insignificant or holding onto grudges. Although adults might do something similar, they have a way of convincing themselves of the other positive things out there. Kids, not so much. If they are fixated on something, well that's it then.

Granted, there is nothing wrong with having a strong and determined mind from an early age. However, it can become a problem if that mind is determined to host negative thoughts. Negative thoughts like body-image issues, lack of confidence, low self-esteem, etc. are things that breed negativity on a large scale. When not discouraged from having such thoughts or paying heed to them, it can land kids in unthinkable trouble in academia, social, and their future professional lives. When they keep submitting to negativity, they rarely focus on the good and, thus, lead a life full of disappointments, heartbreaks, and mental health issues.

What are Negative Thoughts?

Negative thinking is a whirlpool of thoughts that leads to people finding the worst in everything. It also means these people might reduce their expectations so low that their minds only come up with worst-case scenarios. It is like a web, each thought connected with newer thoughts developing every second. Imagine your child has been asked to play a small role in a school play, a small part with almost zero dialogue. All your child has to do is stand on one side, wearing a tree costume. Your child is naturally shy and thinks they will not be able to pull it off.

"Can you tell Ms. Nora that I won't be able to perform in the play?"

"But why?"

"I don't think I can do it. What if I actually make a fool out of myself? What if I vomit or faint on the stage? Everyone will laugh at me. They will call me a loser forever. I will have no friends and no one will ever forget it."

Notice how the child is thinking the worst and each thought is just a continuation of the one before, like a vicious thread? This is what negative thinking looks like. It shatters a child's confidence and makes them believe they are good for nothing. It can manifest in a pattern of worry, stress, and depression over time.

Many kids are prone to negative thinking, leading them to have meltdowns, engage in fights, and make risky decisions. When they are young, they aren't able to comprehend the many thoughts in their head; but as they grow older and reach early adolescence, they begin to make connections. For instance, they learn that the normal behavior to exhibit when sad is crying. They learn that sometimes when they are anxious or stressed, they turn to biting their nails or pacing back and forth. These are all natural reactions to stressful or disturbing situations. However, a reaction is different from a behavior. While the former is more natural, the latter isn't: it is more of a choice. How we choose to behave, address, and process what is going on is referred to as our "behavior:.

To teach any behavior, it has to be repeated enough times that it turns into a habit—something you do unintentionally like putting your hand on your mouth when yawning or closing your eyes when faced with danger or horror. Therefore, as parents, we need to instill such habits in our kids that will automatically help them navigate their way to positivity and optimism.

Negative thinking works on two principles:

It disqualifies the positive, meaning that it dismisses any positive thought or acknowledgment in our head and takes us back to thinking illogically. We only see the negatives with clarity.

It maximizes the negative and minimizes the positive. So, instead of looking at our positive achievements, we magnify our losses and failures, even if small.

There are many ways of negativity manifesting itself. It mostly comes in one or more of the following forms.

Cynicism: the most common that usually denotes a child has a general distrust for people. They have a difficult time listening to people ,who are trying to encourage them and doubt their motives instead.

Hostility: usually prominent in adolescents and teenagers. As their bodies grow, the chemical imbalances and hormonal changes often lead to mood swings. They develop feelings of unfriendliness towards others and become hesitant in opening up or developing new relationships.

Polarized thinking: this way of thinking usually suggests that if a child thinks they are not good at something, say playing the piano or math, then they think they are horrible. They don't believe in being average and don't make any effort to become better at it. It's black or white for them.

Filtering: this is rather self-explanatory. Kids only notice the bad—or worse—they magnify it in their minds.

Jump to Conclusions: some children are quick to assume the worst in things. If something remotely scary comes their way, they take no time in thinking about the worst-case scenarios. They think nothing good can actually come out of a bad situation - ever.

Blaming: kids with negativity corrupting their minds also find it easier to blame others for their own maladies. They often take the role of the victim in everything, thinking nothing fair ever happens to them.

Heaven's reward fallacy: they are staunch believers that if they work hard or sacrifice, they will be rewarded. However, when that reward doesn't come, they take to depression and bitterness. An example looks something like this: your child studies hard for exams and pulls all-nighters. However, when the result is out, they don't score well. So the next time, they don't work hard at all.

Why it's Easy to Just Give Up

Giving up is sometimes the easiest thing to do. As adults, we ourselves are guilty of this habit, so we don't get to simply tell our kids not to. Many people, children included, give up because they can't face the stress and pain associated with something, and they'd rather put an end to their misery. We choose not to endanger our comfort zone and step out to make sacrifices, all for some uncertain future. Doesn't seem like a very wise bargain, does it?

But do you know why we must always bet against the odds? It is because there is one thing more damaging and hurtful, and that is regret. If you don't try, regret will always follow. If you don't encourage your kids to try and never quit, they will always regret it later. It is an unwanted feeling that keeps us stuck in the past. Had I chosen to take that course during my semester break, I would have been promoted. Had I learned a unique skill, it would have helped me get the job. Had I chosen to follow my passion for sports, I could have made a blooming career out of it.

We don't want our children to live with regrets. Let's say they are giving up something because the goal doesn't seem appealing. It is about revising everything taught at school. They say it is too tiring and time-consuming, and they would rather spend their time playing outdoors or a game on their tablet. They promise they will start studying once the finals are near and make it up.

For the following days, they will feel relieved that they don't have to do it anymore. They might even enjoy the free time for a few weeks, but then what? They will have regrets a few months later when they have to study for the finals and spend hours in their room, sunken in their books. Not to mention, the additional stress and pressure of learning about so much in a short period. That is when regret will settle in and make them panic. That is when they will start to hate themselves and a little bit of you, too, for not pushing them hard enough to stick with the studying. Not only that, but they also will not be able to perform their best and pass the class with decent grades.

There are several reasons why kids find giving up easy. Let's discuss a few.

They don't have a strong "Why?"

Did you know that Walt Disney was fired several times, told he had no original ideas and lacked imagination? Had he chosen to give up, we wouldn't have the world of Disney and the amazing shows we grew up watching.

Like Mr. Walt, some kids don't have a compelling reason to keep going. They lack the answer to that "why" that our brain keeps asking as we work towards a goal. When the answer isn't powerful enough, we are likely to give up.

Expecting Fast Results

Some kids, although not suffering from ADHD, just want things to move at a fast pace. They want quick results and are rarely willing to do the work when it comes to something detail-oriented. They are also the ones who resort to taking shortcuts. Shortcuts work, no doubt about that, but not always. And when things don't go as planned, meltdowns and frustration are bound to happen.

As parents, we have to make them patient with a more stable and calm mindset. We must let them know that not all goals can be achieved in a short period and, thus, they must continue to work for them without getting disheartened. Some may have gotten it easy, having things presented to them on a silver plate, but life isn't fair to all, and that is okay. A classic example can be your teenager trying to lose weight to look a certain way but wanting quick results. So, they resort to quick fixes and aren't willing to do the actual work. They starve themselves, boycott all carbs and later complain of dizziness and poor concentration and energy levels.

Presuming They Have Unique Problems

A lot of kids presume that no one will understand what they are going through because their problems are so unique. Oh, really? Are you the first-ever child to be bullied at school? Are you the first-ever human to have been compared to an older sibling or cousin? Are you the first-ever individual to have broken up with a friend or a partner? Kids who assume they have unique problems fail to see the larger picture. They think that what they are going through is something their parents, peers, or friends won't understand. So, they bother not to speak about them or find solutions.

Doubting Capabilities

Some kids just don't find that push within to bring their ideas to fruition. It isn't that they aren't smart; they just lack confidence and believe that they will be ridiculed or made fun of. A lack of confidence in our abilities often halts us from trying new things. Many kids, doubting their skills and abilities, abandon their long-term goals. Here's the thing: if you don't have the right mindset and you are always listening to your inner critic, you will be pushing away a lot of valuable things in life. Therefore, parents have to ensure that our kids don't feel discouraged and fail to fulfill their dreams and aspirations. We have to be their encouragement and that push that makes them want to see what's at the bottom of the cliff, and later dive their way through the crests and troughs of life. We have to remind them how wholesome it can feel to achieve goals and experience the joy that comes with it.

One Failure Wears Them Down

Why are kids so quick to give up, you ask? They think that if they are putting their hearts and souls into something, it should come out right be it a school project, an assignment, or an exam. However, one failure is enough to get them off track and concoct negative thoughts. Failure too can be rewarding. You learn from your mistakes and rethink strategies from a different angle. It piques curiosity and also serves as a motivation to try harder. Besides, achieving something isn't always in the cards. For some kids, it comes a little late while for some it never does. In both these cases, as parents, we have to make them see the bright side of things and prevent them from going into self-doubt.

Kids who are quick to give in whenever they come across the first stumbling block may take more time in training and developing positive habits. But it isn't impossible.

Lack of Self-Discipline and Resilience in Life

Some kids give up easily because they lack the discipline required to stay patient and wait for the rewards. Since they aren't disciplined, they expect quick results. They are soon to judge and give up because according to them, things haven't turned out the way they had wanted and, thus, there really isn't any point further in sticking to working hard. However, the most important lesson is that they must learn to become disciplined and have control over their emotions and feelings.

Chapter 2
Why are Children Insecure?

That's the million-dollar question, right? It's vital to attempt to comprehend the foundation of our kids' uncertainty so we can start to manage it. In this part, we will layout the primary trouble spots for kids. We will examine the elements that lead to low confidence and afterward we start to foster the technique for managing those concerns.

Understanding the Problem

Children are new, unadulterated, pristine, and very touchy about the climate they are encircled with. Through long stretches of managing large numbers of life's hardships, numerous grownups have developed a thicker skin or a superior safeguard component against a portion of those common pressures.

Picture a scratch on your lower arm, with the scratch bearing crude skin to the rest of the world. It reacts to the smallest touch, and an excessive amount of strain can be excruciating. The layers of skin aren't there to give insurance. They are as yet crude skin, and you, as the parent, should secure that crudeness and support it until it is prepared to confront the world on its own.

Parents have a significant impact on their child's social well-being and self-esteem. You can't address it. We are there from the time they are conceived and set out the brickwork of their foundation.

Factors that Influence Self-Esteem in Children

Think of that skin and think about your kids. What kind of elements can make them delicate to their general surroundings? What components in their day-to-day existence are making a negative impact? What are you doing in your kid's life that may be more ruinous than constructive?

I'll respond to that inquiry by showing you a portion of the variables that impact self-esteem:

Body and wellness – both nourishment and exercise are main considerations in the general prosperity of a child.

Rest and unwinding – yes, children genuinely should have down time. Appreciate the association among psyche and body- the relaxation and enthusiasm for the body we have been given.

Negative climate and legitimate articulation – negative encounters and past worries can influence your youngster's self-esteem.

Cultivating positive idea – teaching your kids to be positive is significant in building self-esteem.

A caring supporting relationship with guardians and friends – knowing you have backing and consolation from others goes far toward a higher self-esteem.

These frame my arrangement to help you and your kid accomplish a more elevated level of self-esteem.

Outside Influence

Many of the things that occur in our kid's life influence their degree of confidence. They are regular events that can prompt a lower degree of confidence. The following are fundamental circumstances that fit into this category.

Think of the 11-year-old kid, who is large. His public activity is choked, and he doesn't learn about hanging with friends. His mental self-view isn't positive, and his confidence is affected.

Let's face it – kids commit errors. How we handle them is vital in sustaining higher self-esteem. If we are continually reprimanding them, their self-esteem begins to decrease. This shouldn't be mistaken for appropriate discipline.

If your kid returns home from school one day, donning a recent trend of doing up their shoes, you may investigate it and say, "what the hell?" They will probably let you know that they got the style from one of their friends. This is significant for youngsters particularly between the ages of 6 and 13. They want to be "important for the group" and do what they can to adopt the in thing. This becomes dangerous when the crowd begins to prohibit a kid. Building a kid's mental self-portrait and distinction is essential to keeping something from turning into a problem.

IS your kid is making statements like:

"I'm never going to have the option to do that… "

"I can't do this… "

I'm not sufficient to attempt it… "

I'll never be seriously amazing… "

This is a certain sign that something in their life is creating a poor mental self-portrait, consequently, dropping their self-esteem.

Being presented with a negative, unsupportive climate prompts a negative, confidence-free youngster. Disclosing the circumstance is significant in assisting them with comprehension and managing the situation.

What Parents do Can Hurt

This is the reason you want to play a functioning job – both as an understudy and facilitator in your kid's confidence advancement. The following are a couple of things you may do that bring down a kid's self-esteem.

High assumptions

Excessive criticism

Calling children names like lazy, stupid, useless, etc. Overprotecting or neglecting of children

Not showing acclaim or appreciation

Using mix-ups to build up failures

This is actually only a glimpse of something larger. You can never perceive the circumstances that genuinely influence the prosperity of your kids since with every youngster it contrasts. Nonetheless, furnishing them with a fundamental system lies in a program like mine. Each of the variables I have depicted, alongside the circumstances that happen in our youngsters' lives, can be restricted and managed properly, assuming the guardians have a plan.

Parents are very important!

Chapter 3
A Child Who Gives up too Easily

We live in a harsh world, and with things getting more stringent, kids need to learn all the skills they can to be successful. Although success has different meanings to different people, the skills required are the same. One of them is perseverance and mental strength. Because of their age, kids are naturally impatient, especially when things are not going their way. Because technology has made it possible to get instant gratification, our little one's concentration span and resilience have become even worse.

Why Perseverance Matters

For a while, Tina watched her daughter struggle with a school project. The little girl was getting so frustrated, and eventually, she abandoned ship and left. In her mind, Tina's daughter was probably wondering why she should continue to struggle with something so frustrating, tedious, or painful.

Studies show that people who persevere in trying circumstances do better in most areas of their lives. Their ability to push through discomfort shows they have a higher IQ, more academic intelligence, and are better performers at work. Without perseverance, kids like Tina's daughter may grow up to be quitters as adults. They may quit a job because they find it redundant and boring or because they didn't get the promotion they were eyeing. Their relationships will also suffer because they are likely to end things every time there is a communication breakdown.

Perseverance is a skill like any other. A child who perseveres is confident. They are confident in their ability and know that they can turn things around, even when they don't work out at first. Teaching them these skills helps them improve their concept of self and become comfortable in their ability. Like confidence, perseverance is an abstract concept that kids may not understand, but it's possible to help kids develop this skill. But first, let us examine why kids give up easily.

They are embarrassed: kids are growing, and during this time, they will encounter a lot of situations that leave them feeling dumb. For instance, Tina's daughter might have thought she knew exactly how to go about her school project, but once she encountered a challenge, she realized that maybe she does not know as much as she thought. If she takes this too seriously, she will condemn herself for being dumb and feel embarrassed.

This happens mostly when kids try to bite more than they can chew. If the school project involves a lot of things, Tina's daughter would have had a better chance if she had not looked at the project as a whole, but divided it into different actionable sections. But kids don't do this: in their minds, they have a project that needs to be completed. Sometimes, looking at the project from this perspective can be so overwhelming that they don't start. That is, giving up even before they start.

Your expectations are high: at every stage of development, kids have tasks they can handle and those they can't no matter how hard they try. Always check if the job you are giving your child is age-appropriate. Toddlers may help clear the table, but setting it might be complicated for them. You should shift your expectations to fit what your child can and cannot do. This will help build their confidence.

The opposite is also true. Sometimes, parents shield their kids so much that they fail to give them age-appropriate tasks. For example, pre-teens can help with a lot of chores in the house: they can arrange their closets, cook an egg, and even help with cleaning the house. Kids who are willing to help often suffer when their parents refuse to give them responsibilities. Using a knife may be dangerous, but a pre-teen can handle themselves with care and help you chop tomatoes.

Putting too much emphasis on winning: winning is good, and there is nothing wrong with it, but when we emphasize winning too much, it takes away the fun from the activity. Also, our kids feel like losers unless they are undefeated. This also happens in class and while doing homework. There is nothing wrong with being competitive, but when game night turns into a teary affair because your child didn't win, you need to help them check their expectations. The process should be as enjoyable as the game. Teach your kids to appreciate the process as much as they appreciate winning. If they didn't win, they will have had fun.

Generic praise: when kids do something great, we naturally want to praise them and show we appreciate their effort. However, simply saying "good girl" and "good boy" or "excellent" is traditionally what parents say to their kids. What we don't realize is that "good boy" can easily be undermined by "bad boy," which confuses the child. Is he actually a good boy or a bad boy? If he hears you tell him that he's a bad boy more than he hears good boy, it registers in his mind that he is a bad boy. On special occasions, he is a good boy. This lowers his confidence.

You don't help with emotions: big emotions are overwhelming for kids, and when they don't understand them, they become frustrated and confused. Emotions such as anger and frustration are often those that make us tick. An angry child will yell, hit others, throw a fit, and do whatever it takes to feel better. This behavior does not sit well with parents, and the likelihood of losing our cool is high. And when we do, we become the big bad wolf.

Another challenge that this causes is that when we lose control, we are unable to help our kids with their emotions. Like Aaron and his father, emotions fly high, and the results are a slammed door and two angry people. Although we should not encourage kids to hit, yell, and shout, we must understand that this is their way of expressing their emotions. we must always talk to them about what is appropriate behavior and what is unacceptable.

One of the best ways to deal with this is to help kids name the emotions they are feeling. This shows them that feelings are actually part of life, and it also communicates that these feelings have a name and a proper way to express them. We must help them name the emotion so they learn what it is they are feeling. Next time your child cries, ask them if they are sad or feeling frustrated.

How to Build Resilience in Kids

Stacy has been picking Tom from school for a while. Things have improved, and he seemed to be doing a lot better. Today, however, she notices that something is off from the moment Tom walks out of the school. He must be upset about something.

"What's wrong, buddy? Are you ok?"

"I got an actual role in the school play."

"That's wonderful! Congratulations!"

"No! No! No! It's not wonderful!"

"Why not?"

"The drama teacher is making me play a girl!" and he bursts into tears.

At this point, Stacy is tempted to laugh, but she understands that her son's emotions are real. He is disappointed, and she acknowledges that. But she keeps quiet.

Go against your instincts: any parent's first instinct would be to talk to Tom about why the situation is not so bad. You would be tempted to come up with three to four reasons why he should not be disappointed, why this is a great opportunity, and even add how much fun it would be. That's our instinct. When we chill with our friends, that's what we do. But the truth is, we talk too much! We tend to explain, analyze, and rationalize everything, which is actually the exact opposite of what our kids need.

Children can't hear information, tactics, and processes when upset: to be honest, neither can you. Think of a time you were upset about something and all you wanted to do was vent. If someone told you that you shouldn't be upset because of 1, 2, and 3 - or what a wonderful learning experience it was - it might upset you further rather than make you feel better. So, why do we do this to our kids? Sitting with your child when they are upset shows you love them, respect what they are feeling, and are ready to offer them a shoulder to cry on. It's incredibly hard for parents to do because our instinct is to protect our little ones. But if we want the best results, we must learn to swim against the current.

Stop saving the day: how many times have you really wanted to save the day when your child comes home upset? Stacy, for instance, could have decided to talk to the drama teacher and ask him to change Tom's role. Would it have made Tom happy? Absolutely! But it would have taught him that his mother will always be there to save him when unpleasant things happen.

Instead of being a super mom, Stacy could use this opportunity to help Tom develop some internal grit. Resilience is developed when we don't quit at first sight of a challenge. To encourage him, she can tell Tom that directors start by awarding smaller roles, but when they see how good an actor is, they can easily swap the role with something more meaningful. If the actor's attitude is positive, it makes the process even easier. Also, the opportunity to make new friends has just been presented. It would be fun to get to know some of the other boys and girls in the play and have fun while at it.

Challenges are a test to your child's emotional immune system. When a healthy body catches a virus, tons of antibodies are produced to help fight the "enemy", and the body becomes stronger. The same happens with resilience. The more your child overcomes challenges, the tougher they grow and the more confident they are that they can solve whatever difficulty they face.

Breakdown the goals: when kids start a project, it's usually all fun until they encounter a roadblock. Let's assume you brought a new puzzle home, and although your little one is excited to give it a go, they are not sure where to start. It's a new challenge for them, and the pieces are much smaller than the ones he is accustomed to. If you notice they are tempted to give up, you could break down the task by asking them if they prefer to look for the corners first. Once that's done, you can move to the edges.

Give failure a new meaning: everyone, including adults, fears falling short. That's completely understandable, but the way life is designed, we are bound to fail every so often. You must talk to your child about failure, and give it a new meaning. If they are learning how to spell, tell them it's natural to get it wrong the first few times, but the more they practice, the better they become. This helps them appreciate the process and enjoy the sweet victory that comes with persistence. Your child will also get a lot of experience with win/lose situations, giving them the confidence they need to keep trying even when they know they might fail.

Use the batman effect: a study conducted on child development shows that asking kids to pretend to be Batman, Dora the Explorer, or other hard-working characters they admire can significantly help them increase their confidence and resilience. The research found that asking kids to embody the characteristics of a hard-working, confident, resilient character helped them to get through the task. These kids were less stressed and managed to perform better than kids who referred to themselves. Next time your child is about to give up, remind him how batman was in the same situation and help him remember how batman made it through. Then ask him to be batman and use batman powers to do the task.

Model the character: kids naturally do what they see us do, not what we tell them to do. Allowing your kids to see you struggle with tasks and not give up shows that they too can handle challenges. Openly tell them when something seems difficult for you but assure them you will not give up. Once you manage, celebrate with them. This could be anything from learning to cook using a new recipe, learning how to play a musical instrument, or completing a project at work.

Chapter 4
What Negativity Does to Your Child?

Do you know who the biggest criticizers of your kids are? Themselves. They can and will do enough damage to themselves if the negative self-talk doesn't stop. We have to teach them how not to let their inner critic prevent them from harm. The reason negative thoughts aren't ever welcoming is that they bring forth emotions like anger, frustration, and stress. It may take you hours to convince them why they should look at the positive aspect of things but only a second for their inner critic to change their mind about it. The only way we can stop them is by identifying negative or harmful behaviors, which means that it has already done some of the fundamental damage. This means that as parents, we have to gear up and teach them how to look past their failures, losses, and have an optimistic mindset.

The Effects of Negativity on Our Minds and Bodies

During one study, researchers found that negative thinking is linked with an increased risk of developing mental health issues. This means that kids who are brought up in an environment that offers them no opportunities to grow, be positive and achieve their dreams with determination are likelier to suffer from mental health issues later in life (Kinderman, Schwannauer, Pontin, & Tai, 2013). Furthermore, it can have some negative effects on the mind and body.

For instance, it can trigger hopelessness. Kids experience decreased motivation and the willpower to continue with something important. They are sure of their loss from the start. This feeling of hopelessness makes an easy task seem and combined with a lack of motivation and drive leads to negative thoughts clouding the mind.

Negative thoughts also limit a child's thought process and problem-solving skills. They keep listening to that inner voice that takes immense pleasure in reminding them things they aren't capable of instead of the ones they are. This limits their thinking to reason creatively and step out of their comfort zones to give something challenging a try.

Kids prone to negative thinking also believe that perfection is attainable. Although not entirely accomplishable, perfection can be a great booster to help kids aim higher. However, studies suggest that focusing too much on it can lead to increased stress. Think about it this way: your child wishes to impress their new art teacher with a sketch. They want it to be perfect, so they spend more time working on it. However, every time they look at it, the more problems they find. They keep going back and forth revising and redrawing it.

A perfectionist can never be happy with what they have and tries to keep improving it. It can be quite addictive and stressful, especially for young kids. Children with a negative outlook about life are also depressed (Schimelpfening, 2020). When left unchecked, little bouts of temporary depression can become quite damaging. And how can we forget that the biggest and most pressing issue with negative thinking is that it isn't positive self-talk? Simplistic as it is, there is tons of research that positive self-talk results in good academia, a successful career, healthier well-being, and meaningful relationships (Tod, Hardy, & Oliver, 2011).

And to provide you with a rather interesting research study involving 400,000 white people and 300,000 Chinese-Americans, researchers in San Diego were astonished to look at the findings. It all began when some researchers looked at the death records of the said amount of randomly-selected white people and Chinese Americans (Philips, Ruth & Wagner, 1993). They found that Chinese Americans died earlier than most white Americans. As it turns out, the Chinese Americans with a combination of an ill-fated birth year (as per the Chinese astrology and medicine) and disease died five years earlier than the rest.

Researchers further dug into the causes of their deaths and concluded that the more strongly the Chinese Americans believed in the Chinese superstitions about the ill-fated birth year, the sooner they died. The reduction in their life expectancy wasn't explainable by genetic factors, their behavior, lifestyle choices, or the skills of the doctors treating their respective diseases. They were dying younger not due to the disease or their flawed genes but due to their strong negative beliefs. They believed that since the stars had hexed them, they were doomed to die earlier. It was nothing but their negative attitude towards life that led them to their ultimate deaths. Quite literally!

What we must notice here is the strong connection between the human brain and body. Negative emotions and stress are becoming two of the most important causes of diseases worldwide. Negativity leads to chronic stress which weakens the heart and impairs the functioning of other organs such as the lungs, kidneys, and also liver. When the body is under constant stress, it loses its balance. It becomes harder to digest and takes more time for us to heal. This makes resting difficult, and the lack of rest and sleep brings more problems to the table.

Putting an end to it for Good

How can we as parents help our young people break this cycle of negativity and stop paying attention to that inner critic? We, being the role models and idols they look up to, can contribute in more than one way to help them in this tough time. But as they say, practice what you preach, and it has to start with you. If your child looks up to a parent who is always nagging about the lack of things, blaming others for their problems, and treating every new opportunity as an obstacle or challenge, they are going to pick up the same vibe. If they see you complaining, they will complain too. If they see you being negative, they will have a negative outlook on things too. If they see you giving up your dreams because of the fear of failure or "what others will say," they won't have the guts to try something new either.

To change them, you have to change yourself first. You will have to embrace positivity and optimism because that is how healthy habits form. Whether you accept it or not, they are going to take after you and take up the habits they see you practicing. So, be the right kind of role model for your kids first and then preach the power of positive thinking.

Say Positive Things to Them

As a parent, you have to help them see the positive in everything especially when they fail at something. You have to point out the good in every circumstance whether they like it or not. The idea is to get them thinking whether the outcome can be positive in some way or not. Once they start to give positive thinking a chance, it will become easier in the long-run. Ideally, you should radiate positivity. It allows children to actually see that there is another, more promising way of looking at things that doesn't end with frustration and sadness.

Teach Them About the Monkey Mind

Monkey Mind is an approach to viewing and processing things. It originates from the Zen concept and suggests that since our brain works tirelessly all day long, transitions from one idea to another, listens to endless chatter both from the internal and external world, craves things and becomes judgmental, it is very easy to get confused. So much happens in the mind that it leaves the little one confused as to what to listen to what thoughts to discard. The brain of a monkey functions in the same manner, says Dr. Arnold who introduced the concept to the world. He goes on to suggest that negative thoughts are like a monkey, climbing from one tree to another. This hinders focus on important tasks. For instance, when kids want to focus on some tasks at hand, they often become distracted. Things like procrastination, a lack of focus, external distractions like noise, chatter, and people around make it harder to concentrate. All these things when amalgamated leads to negative thinking. First, procrastination delays the process, then a lack of focus makes simple tasks appear difficult, and next external noises and chatter just add more pressure on the kids. Thus, they give up the task altogether.

So how to stop the monkey from climbing one tree after another and giving up everything important because it seems hard? Dr. Arnold believes that to flip negative thinking, we must direct kids to follow these three steps.

Take a deep breath

Tell yourself to "stop and relax" sternly

Chant something positive to yourself like, "I got this" or "I can handle it."

This simple exercise can help kids break the chain of negative thoughts and replace them with something positive.

Keep a Gratitude Journal

Gratitude journals or simply listing down five things you are grateful for in life is a great way to keep the mind focused on the positive in our lives. Make it a routine to encourage the habit of keeping a gratitude journal or reminding your kids to count their blessings before going to bed so it is the last thing they remember and wake up feeling positive and motivated.

If they aren't too keen on maintaining a gratitude journal, simply ask them to write their thoughts in a diary, a vessel to pour in their feelings. Haven't we all felt a whole lot better after discussing our problems and worries with someone? However, since most kids feel shy about taking their problems to their parents, this can work in their favor and prevent the frustration and negative thinking that builds up inside. When they are made to feel grateful for the things they have, it changes the way they think and views things. They start to approach things with a new sense of positivity and elevated motivation.

Problem-Solve With Them

Keep in mind that there is a big difference between problem-solving with them and for them. You have to help them come up with solutions or lead them with hints on how to do things so they don't give up on them easily. For instance, if they are doing a puzzle, you can guide them by asking them to put a certain piece to check if it fits. The idea is to help them but also make them think that they came up with it on their own. Not only does this encourage them to keep attempting and trying, but it also instills a sense of victory in them. It actually makes them feel confident in their abilities and with time, makes them self-reliant.

Empathize

Knowing that others understand what they are going through is another way to lessen the impact of negative thinking. Empathizing with your child allows you to show that feeling a certain way is completely normal. It makes them feel heard and understood. When kids feel heard and cared for, they feel more supported and become more willing to give things another try in case they didn't work out the first time. For instance, saying things like, "I know you must be feeling like a complete failure to not have caught that ball in the game, but you aren't one. You will catch it the next time," can be motivating.

Switch Perspectives

"What would your favorite athlete or celebrity do if they were in this rut?"

Teaching kids to think from someone else's perspective gives their problems a new meaning and visualization. For example, if they are a fan of some rock star or footballer, ask them what they would have done in this situation. Not only does that offer some form of positive distraction, but it also helps kids try to come up with solutions on their own. After all, they wouldn't want to disappoint their favorite character. If they still seem unconvinced, ask them if their favorite rock star would have said, "I quit" too?

Chapter 5
How Children's Confidence Changes with Age

We may learn about the origins of selfhood via clever experiments, such as covertly putting a dot of rouge on a child's nose and then placing the toddler in front of a reflection. When they see the dot in the mirror, very young toddlers will reach for the mirror, but by the time they are eighteen months old, they identify themselves in the glass and will massage the bridge of their nose when they see the dot. Having a feeling of who they are as a person suggests they are confident. Also, they have a sense of what is normal for them and what is not, at least in terms of physical appearance.

During the period between the ages of eighteen and twenty-seven months, youngsters begin to utter "I," "me," "my," and the delightful word "mine!" The opposite is true for toddlers, who refuse to judge themselves. The author Susan Harter has conducted hundreds of interviews with children of all ages to get insight into how children see and assess themselves. Based on her findings, I've listed and explained the major developmental phases below so you can see what's usual for children of various ages.

It is important to understand these phases because they will provide you with an overview of the natural ups and downs in self-confidence that youngsters encounter throughout childhood. It is possible that a child's poor self-confidence is the result of a long-term trend; however, this is not always the case. When you know what's normal, you can put yourself in your child's shoes and comprehend what they're experiencing. There is a wide range of ages connected with each stage. You may discover that your kid is a bit ahead of or a little below a developmentally expected growth pattern. As you go through the phases of self-confidence, you'll notice that the concepts of connection, competence, and choice reoccur. When it comes to relationships and feeling competent, children of all ages have strong feelings.

Self-Confidence for Preschoolers

Most preschoolers are lovable little show-offs, with the exception of a few highly self-conscious young toddlers who despise being the center of attention. The majority have reached what I refer to as the "look at me!" stage. They have a strong sense of self-worth because they are unable to objectively assess themselves. They make exaggerated statements such as "I'm so quick!" or "I know all my ABCs," even though they realize they are not correct. They like having an audience for their actions, and while they bounce about the room, they shout things like, "Watch me do my huge leaps!" and other such things.

Kids of this age are actually very sensitive to the emotions of adults. When grownups compliment them, they burst out laughing and pump out their chests with delight. On the other hand, they tremble in humiliation when reprimanded or fail to complete a job successfully. At this point, children do not express their thoughts about themselves verbally, but their self-confidence may be seen in the way they conduct themselves. They may be apprehensive about exploring new territory or avoiding obstacles. When under difficulty, they may weep and give up readily. They may seem unconcerned with their job rather than enthusiastic about it. These are things that all children do from time to time. Unless they are part of a regular, continuous trend, they aren't cause for alarm.

Support Your Children Curiosity

By supporting our children's curiosity and desire to try new things, as well as by expressing satisfaction in their successes, we may help them build their self-confidence throughout the look-at-me! period. We are under no obligation to agree with their assessments that they are the best, but we are allowed to express our opinions on their effort, strategy, pleasure, and growth. We may say things like, "You didn't stop until you colored the entire thing! That's good" or "You worked hard until you colored the whole thing!" or "You have a genuine passion for jumping!" or "Wow! The things you're doing are becoming more and more precise!"

When dealing with young children that misbehave, we must also be kind to them. Redirecting children toward what they should be doing is both nicer and more successful than scolding or punishing them when it comes to teaching youngsters the appropriate things to do. Despite the fact that these young children are unable to verbalize views about their own self-confidence, they are starting to develop an understanding of themselves as competent or unable, beloved or unlovable, based on their interactions with adults and other children.

Self-Confidence for Five-to-Seven-Year-Old Children

The next level is what I refer to as the "I'm on my way" stage. Because they want to compare what they can accomplish today to what they could do a year or two ago, children in the early elementary school years often have high self-confidence because they can see a significant improvement in their abilities. This is a stage in which skills are quickly developing. Six-year-olds are much better than four-year-old at riding a bike, reading and writing words, doing elementary algebra, playing board games, and throwing a ball with pinpoint precision.

These significant shifts are exhilarating for children! Kids of this age are very concerned with the concept of fairness. They compare themselves to others mostly to determine whether or not they are being treated fairly rather than to assess their own performance. On-my-way stage children recognize that they are being judged by others and begin to create opinions about themselves as being excellent or awful at specific activities.

In general, they still have an unreasonably high level of confidence in their own skills. Despite the fact that children at this age do not express feelings of overall self-worth, a new study has shown that even children as young as five have a broad awareness of their own unique attributes. If they realize they are far behind other children in the development of key talents, such as reading or swimming, their self-confidence may suffer.

Kids this age are known for being inflexible thinkers as they attempt to navigate their rapidly growing surroundings. They remark things like, "That's babyish!" Simple either-or categories make the world simpler to comprehend, but they also lead to strong ideas about what they actually do or don't want to do, as well as what other children should or shouldn't do. Children whose interests do not conform to stereotypes may find it difficult to fit in.

At this age, friendship is a significant contributor to their sense of self-worth. When children are in their early elementary years, they are extremely concerned with having friends, but they are not very good at being friends because they have difficulty imagining how others feel. They perform well one minute and then disagree the next. They may have a close friend, but their relationships with other people are generally shaky. They're typically demanding and judgmental, yet when somebody criticizes or rejects them, their emotions are readily wounded.

Kids this age are prone to cheating or quitting in a huff when things aren't going their way in a game or activity. Also, they're more likely to tell a lie to avoid getting into trouble (although it is typically clear when they do that).

Children in elementary school, as opposed to younger children, have created a sense of self based on their personal history, which includes incidents from the past that are relevant to their present position and have consequences for their future. In addition, primary school youngsters like daydreaming about their future careers, which may include being an astronaut, actor, or a renowned rock star - perhaps all at the same time - and ideally performing all of these things with their pals! At this age, warning indicators of prospective difficulties with low self-confidence include not being able to define something they are good at or not expressing an ambition for the future, among other things.

Children who frequently refer to themselves as "stupid," "mean," or "bad," as well as those who appear sad, irritable, or unenergetic, require assistance in addressing their low self-confidence. As parents, the most effective strategy to help our children build their self-confidence throughout the on-my-way period is to assist them in learning new abilities and be excited about their development. These children are very concerned about pleasing their parents.

Furthermore, we must ensure they have plenty of opportunities to socialize with friends. Friendships are formed via one-on-one playdates that take place outside of school. When a disagreement arises, we may assist our children in reaching a resolution or providing a diversion by asking a timely question such as, "Who wants a snack?", to help them get through the difficult period.

Self-Confidence for Eight-to-Ten-Year-Old Children

Many youngsters have challenges with their self-confidence at the age of eight to ten, during the era of assessing themselves. The ability to accurately compare oneself to others has evolved in youngsters by this age; when they recognized that they are not always the greatest at what they do, it is a sign of progress in their development. The consequence is that they tend to perceive themselves in a more negative light than younger children do, and they may have feelings of inadequacy.

Kids at this age are often tough on themselves. They're acutely aware of the disparity between their ideal selves and the reality of their lives. It's difficult for them to understand the concept that learning is a process and developing abilities takes time. If they are not instantly successful at anything, they may come to the conclusion that they are "no good" at that particular activity.

Kids in the judging-myself stage may also engage in defensive behavior to safeguard their self-confidence. It is common to say things like "I'm terrible at sports, but I don't care!" Or "Sports are a waste of time!". When someone is putting up their best effort at something they are failing to understand or do, they may feel vulnerable.

Children realize that they may have both good and bad characteristics at the same time when in the judging-myself stage, but it might be a warning sign if they focus mostly on their faults and think they have few positive characteristics to balance them out.

They may engage in a range of harmful behaviors to boost their self-confidence. Some youngsters, for example, attempt to make themselves feel better by putting others down. Some spend their time mostly with children they can control or impress. Others, on the other hand, grow furious. The use of one or more of these harmful coping mechanisms on a regular basis might be a symptom of poor or unstable self-confidence. We may help our children's self-confidence by trying to temper their harsh judgements while they are in this period of development. In response to our child's cry of "I can't do anything well!" we might remark, "You're having difficulties with this activity right now."

Our words might encourage them to keep trying or our trust in their ability to sort things out if they persevere. On top of this, we may assist them in acknowledging their achievements. In the event they make a mistake, we should offer them the opportunity to make it right. We want them to see a way forward rather than feeling trapped in their "badness." The stories of our past struggles can be inspiring and reassuring to children at this age, as they typically look up to their parents.

Self-Confidence in Teens

The middle school years, between the ages of eleven and thirteen, I refer to as the "trying to look nice stage." During this time, children are often acutely self-conscious, and their self-confidence is generally lower than it was during stages of development. They are preoccupied with what other people think of them and where they stand in the social hierarchy. When asked whether they are awful at arithmetic, younger children may respond, "I am!" However, middle school students are more likely to respond, "My math instructor despises me!" when the math teacher has just reminded them to turn in their work.

Body changes associated with puberty—or the absence of such changes—increase self-consciousness throughout the trying-to-look-good period of a person's life. These children are very concerned with seeming "normal," and they say their self-confidence is mostly determined by how they feel about their physical appearance. In front of the mirror, they are known to spend a significant amount of time analyzing and scrutinizing every inch of their looks. And it isn't only girls who have a vast list of perceived physical faults to be ashamed of. Boys are becoming more focused with their physical appearance—for example, desiring to have "six-pack abs"—and are acutely aware of how much they fall short of what they perceive to be the physical ideal in society.

Because children of this age are consumed with assessing every tiny detail of their appearance and behavior, they imagine that other people are similarly preoccupied. They are under the impression that everyone is continuously staring at them. They may attempt to blend in by wearing and behaving precisely like the other members of their social group to seem normal. They may spend a significant amount of time worrying about potential social blunders. While all of this concern about what others think may seem frivolous or exaggerated to adults, research indicates that for early adolescents, the views of their peers may have serious effects on their personal and social lives.

As a result, telling young teenagers, "Don't be concerned about what other people think!" does not make sense. That just isn't doable for them at this time. You should ask instead, "Are these individuals' opinions important to you?" Do you have confidence in their judgement? Do they have a significant influence on your life?" Questions like these might help your youngster have a better awareness that various individuals may have diverse points of view and not all viewpoints are equally legitimate or valuable.

Because children's self-confidence is so heavily reliant on understanding, remembering, estimating, or predicting the emotions of others at this time may swing rapidly up and down from one extreme to the other. They go from feeling intelligent and cool to feeling foolish and embarrassed in the blink of an eye. The support of close friends and family members might assist to mitigate these mood changes.

Texting, online gaming, and social media activities are all common among middle-school students, and they get more intense in high school. New concerns, including identity theft and cyberbullying, are emerging but for the vast majority of children, online activities serve to strengthen and expand their existing face-to-face connections. It may be quite reassuring for children to know that their pals are literally only a few inches away in their back pockets.

An investigation into the social media activity of thirteen-year-olds recently discovered that 84%believe that social media makes them feel good about themselves at least sometimes, and only 19% believe that social media makes them feel bad about themselves - at least sometimes. Social media provides children with an opportunity to convey a favorable picture of themselves to the rest of the world. For self-conscious tweens and adolescents, on the other hand, it means hey will be subjected to a whole new degree of public exposure as well as a limitless number of opportunities to compare themselves to others. Some people may feel that "everyone else" has a lot more fascinating and engaging existence than they do, which may be debilitating.

We also know that accessing social media on a regular basis is associated with being in distress. The exact cause of this increase in social media checking is unclear; it is possible that unhappy children check social media more frequently as a result of being unhappy, or that another factor such as shyness or loneliness contributes to both increased distress and increased social media checking.

In the trying-to-look-good period, red flags might include a lack of supporting friends as well as an unpleasant self-consciousness that causes children to avoid being in the company of their peers. Another issue to be concerned about is when online activity takes precedence over face-to-face engagement with peers. Children at this age value connections with peers even more than they did when they were younger, as their developing sense of independence becomes more essential to them.

Relationships with parents, on the other hand, do not diminish in significance. We are still very important to our children—in a big way. You may play a critical role in fostering genuine self-confidence in your kid at this point by assisting him or her in finding fun activities and organizations to participate in together. As a counterbalance to some of the shallow ideals and unrealistic standards that saturate popular culture, you may be a powerful force for good.

It is important to remind your kid that it is illogical to compare how she feels on the inside with how someone else seems on the outside. Your kid will find comfort in your constant presence, as well as the knowledge that you watch her with loving eyes, despite the fact that she may ignore your words.

The trying-to-be-myself stage occurs between the ages of fourteen and sixteen, and it is known to be a particularly tough era for children in terms of self-confidence. Teens at this age spend a significant amount of time attempting to determine who they "truly" are. Being concerned about seeming fake, they are extremely concerned about the fact that their behavior differs when they are with others or in different settings.

Trying to discern if they are really nice or harsh, gregarious or quiet, industrious or lazy, they worry over the decision. They consider themselves to be intricate and one-of-a-kind. They are often under the impression that no one, particularly their parents, can comprehend what they are saying. We begin to see significant disparities in the incidence of depression between boys and girls at this point in their schooling.

Beginning about the age of thirteen, rates of depression in girls—but not in boys—start to rise dramatically. Girls are actually twice as likely as males to be depressed by the time they reach late adolescence. Although it is usual for teenagers of this age to be gloomy or aloof with their parents, acting in this manner around peers may be reason for worry.

Depressive symptoms in teens include feeling sad or irritable most of the time, feeling worthless, experiencing excessive or inappropriate guilt, being tired all the time or having noticeably less energy, losing interest in activities they actually used to enjoy, having difficulty concentrating, and/or experiencing changes in sleep, weight, or appetite.

Make it possible for your kid to experiment with multiple personas while still insisting on acceptable boundaries to keep your youngster safe. If you must discipline your kid, do it kindly and provide an opportunity to make apologies. Avoid bringing up anything your child did more than a month ago since kids at this age are trying hard to build a new sense of self and don't want to be burdened by their errors or infantile comments or acts. Instead, focus on your child's current achievements. It's also best not to make any bad predictions regarding your child's life. It is harsh and unhelpful to tell or suggest to teenagers, "Get it together, or you'll never do anything in your life!" This is especially true for girls. Demonstrate unflinching confidence in your child's ability to pick the route that is best for him or her. Provide a safe haven from which your kid may launch his or her adventures, as well as a source of consolation amid the inevitable hard patches.

Self-Confidence in Young Adulthood

The age of seventeen is a watershed moment in a child's self-confidence. Self-contradictions that were so concerning for younger kids are less concerning for older teens because they perceive themselves as more complicated, multidimensional individuals with more complex personalities. They realize and accept that it is possible to be both outgoing and timid at the same time, depending upon the context, and that this is normal. Additionally, since they have a deeper understanding of who they are and what is important to them, their self-confidence is less reliant on how other people see them.

Average self-confidence levels begin to rise in our mid-to-late twenties and then again in our fifties and sixties before beginning to decline by the time we reach the age of seventy, according to research. Unfortunately, telling a youngster or adolescent who is battling with low self-confidence, "Don't worry! You're not alone!" is not really consoling.

General Trends and Your Particular Child

In addition to overall developmental tendencies, there are individual variances among individuals of the same age that must be taken into consideration. Long-term research has shown that children who have lower self-confidence relative to their classmates at a young age are more likely to experience lower self-confidence at an older age as well. Once they've built a mental image of how others see them, that picture shapes their behavior as well as their interpretation of other people's reactions to them. They have a tendency to think and behave in ways consistent with their initial self-perception. In the event that they anticipate being rejected, they will be on the watch for indicators of rejection and will make little effort to be nice. If people believe they will fail, they will refrain from attempting. Their self-criticism might become a self-fulfilling prophecy if they don't take action.

self-confidence in children is often unreasonably high while they are very young and then gradually declines throughout school, with obvious dips at the age of eight and in the early to mid-adolescent years. That decline in children's self-confidence occurs at the same time as an increase in self-focus, and I don't believe it is a coincidence. As children get older, their self-perceptions become more nuanced, they devote more time to contemplating and analyzing themselves, and they tend to become more self-critical. (By contrast, the rising duties and responsibilities of adults tend to direct their focus outward, toward family, colleagues, customers, the community, social causes, and other issues.) If children's self-confidence is on a decreasing trend, does it indicate parents must work hard to raise their self-confidence? No.

Chapter 6
Factors that Affect Self-Confidence

Leading By Example

Before getting down to the actual business of helping your child develop ultimate self- confidence, it is critical to consider your own level of confidence. Your child watches you very carefully, even when you are not looking. He or she will become a sum of who you are, no matter how you might tell your child to do things differently than you. When you act self-confident, your child will naturally emulate confidence. This is wonderfully helpful when you feel assured of your personal capabilities to meet life's demands. On the other hand, if you lack an appropriate amount of confidence, your child will also end up lacking this important quality.

A Confident Environment

Just as flowers grow best with the right amount of sunlight, your child is going to grow the most self-confident if you create an environment that supports maturing. For this, it's important to keep in mind that self-confidence is a belief in one's capabilities. Consider your child's daily routine and consistently seek ways to allow the child to become more capable of caring for him or herself and less dependent on you. This may require step stools in the bathroom and kitchen so your child can reach the sink or after school snacks, for instance.

While providing new ways for your child to assume more responsibility for his or her daily routine, eliminate all forms of sarcasm or hurtful criticism. Your child will fail, and that does not matter. What matters is that your child is making efforts. Be a cheerleader, even if things do not go quite as planned. Being a cheerleader means that you point out the positive yet do not become dishonest or always say, "That is GREAT!" if it is not great. At the same time, you can find something positive to point out about the efforts he or she is making.

Along with being your child's cheerleader, you want to be a helper for problem solving, without being the problem-solver yourself. An example is if your child spills the milk. Instead of criticizing, you could say, "I see the milk got spilled, how do you think you should clean it up?" When your child chooses to get a towel to clean up, you can let him or her know what a great idea it was. Do you see how this will instill confidence in his or her capabilities? Allow your child to clean up the mess. You can always go back later for a more thorough cleaning when the child is not around.

Physical Activities that Boost Self-Confidence

As a quick experiment, adjust your posture so you are sitting up straight with your head erect, shoulders relaxed away from your ears and slightly back, and your spine elongated. Now, put a smile on your face. Consider how much more confident you feel when you have great posture and a pleasant face. Your child will also feel more confident with great posture and a smiling face. In fact, just having good posture prompts a physiological response that relieves stress and creates a feeling of empowerment. This response naturally equates to increased self-confidence.

Enrolling your child in physical activities or just playing outside with him or her are ways to encourage a more empowered posture. You can also make a game of standing up straight and tall by walking with books on your head. It is important to find physical activity that your child enjoys so he or she will become motivated to pursue it without prompting. School sports, running, dance, martial arts, cycling or skating are all great ideas. Ideally, your child will get at least one hour per day of physical activity.

Having good posture and a fit body from staying active will promote self-confidence in ways that nothing else will. For extra measure, make sure there is an abundant amount of time spent outdoors. Vitamin D from the sun will boost your child's mood. Happiness and feelings of wellbeing always promotes confidence.

Chapter 7
The Real Power of Self-Confidence

Let me clue you in on a secret. It is a secret because a lot of people don't like to admit this. The secret is that most people are unsure and lack confidence. Now, don't get too excited. Lacking conviction does not necessarily mean that they have absolutely no self-confidence. They lack enough confidence. In other words, it's below the level they need to live their lives at peak performance.

Now, this revelation is quite apparent. You just examine all the lives of the people you know, and I can guarantee you that 80% of the time, they are living below their fullest potential. In other words, they are capable of so much more yet settle for a life several levels below that full potential. They're paying and taking second place. They're not venturing forth to the fullest extent of what they are capable of getting out of life.

Again, the reason for this is that they lack confidence. They are not confident enough. This is why people who possess self-confidence at high levels are very magnetic. People who lack confidence are drawn to sure people. It's easy to see the positive aspect: it's effortless to see people who are drawn to you, and they encourage you. The bottom line, whether they say it or not, is that I'm attracted to you because you have something that I don't have at a high enough level.

However, you can also draw people in the wrong ways. Some people lack confidence, and they know it, so they try to attack, expose, or put on the spot people who are naturally more confident than them. There is always that variation. Whatever form it takes, confident people are "magnetic" precisely because they make people around them feel comfortable. Again, there is negative magnetism because people can sometimes be envious of what you have. They want to be comfortable, but they think they have to attack you because they think that's the only way they can make up for their lack of confidence.

Regardless, when you're confident, you're automatically magnetic. Sure people fulfil other people's perception or wish for comfort and support. In other words, people around you are looking for leadership. They're like lost sheep looking for a shepherd. I know that sounds insulting because when you say to someone's face that he is acting like a sheep, don't be surprised if you get a fist in your mouth.

But that's the truth: people at some level or another lack enough confidence, and they know this. They naturally gravitate toward people with a healthy level of readily visible and readily detected self-confidence. Why does this happen? Why are people looking for leadership? Well, confident people make those around them feel things are possible. This is the mark of leadership. When you make people around you think that certain things are possible, they can't get enough of you. Left to their own devices or left to themselves, they think things are harder than they are. They think that things are not easy and there are many obstacles along the way.

When you come around and inspire them, and they feel that things are possible, they can't help but sit up and pay attention. You make them think the specific things they can't usually think on their own. If you hang around long enough with confident people, they get others to think that things are not only possible but probable. This is what people are actually looking for in leadership and in their social circles.

Have you ever noticed groups of teenagers and that some of them are more aggressive than others? Well, when you take a group of teenage boys, who are otherwise usually timid, and throw in there a leader of the same age who motivates them to do certain things, you'd be surprised as to what that group can do. Of course, this can play out either positively or negatively.

A lot of the hooligan violence and gang violence you hear about in the news usually involve groups of teenagers with a leader or two that push them to feel that certain things are probable. Steal from a liquor store? Well, if the leader is not in the mix, then that's just an idle fantasy. Once you throw in the right person in their midst, it's only a matter of time until the group knocks over a liquor store.

You see how this works? It can play out positively or negatively. But the truth cannot be denied that confident people get others around them to feel that things are not only possible but probable. I don't actually know about you, but that is the definition of power.

Chapter 8
The Power of the Parent

With great power comes great responsibility, right? As parents, we are given total control. We're the sole person responsible for the survival of this little human. The older we get, the more in control they become, and that's when things get tricky. It's easy to know how to change a diaper and feed a baby a bottle. Sure, there are explosions in public with only one wipe left in the bag, and the screams for food are exhausting. So is explaining to your child why it's not ok for them to draw on the face of their sibling with a permanent marker you forgot you had in your purse. As parents, it is our responsibility to do the best we can all of the time. But how do we really know what is best? How can we figure out a way to raise a child when we still have those moments of struggle just caring for ourselves?

One of the most essential things you can do for your kid is to help them develop their own self-esteem and self-confidence. Create a mindset for them where they are the superhero, able to resolve any issues that come their way. We need to ensure that our kids know they are smart, worthy, and capable. The more you can build this within them, the easier it will be to manage the messy side of parenting. Kids need you to survive well into adulthood, but they don't have to depend on you.

Raising a confident kid means nurturing one who can make their own decisions. They will be able to motivate themselves and push through the challenging moments on their own. They will know right from wrong and have the self-esteem to strive for the best. They will have passion, originality, and empathy. There are going to be instances of trauma that you won't be able to control. Things like divorce, the death of a family member, and bullying from classmates might still occur. It is your job as a parent to ensure that you aren't contributing to this trauma. You don't want to be the reason that your child struggles with who they are as a person. To begin this journey, you need to dive deep into what confidence means to you and reiterate the underlying reasons why it is so important to instill in your beloved child.

Is Confidence Natural?

Much of the thoughts and feelings we have sometimes feel natural. It's natural to scream when you're scared. It's natural to laugh when something funny happens. It is natural to cry when you are sad. One thing we might question whether it is inherent to our biological makeup or not is confidence. You might wonder if you lack confidence, will that mean that your child will as well?

There are a few different things we have to understand about confidence. First and foremost, genetics plays a partial role in determining the level of confidence you experience. For example, if you are predisposed to having something like anxiety or depression, among other mental illnesses, this could potentially pass down to your child, prohibiting their ability to have a healthy level of natural self-esteem (Mayo Clinic, n.d.). But it does not mean that just because a parent lacks confidence, their child will. Confidence is something that helps sustain our level of necessary self-esteem. We have to be naturally confident to a certain degree because self-assurance tells us it's okay to be who we are, capable of accomplishing everything and anything that comes our way.

If you don't have confidence, it inhibits your ability to achieve greatness. Some things happen by chance, and others might be given to us because of circumstances. However, much of what comes into our lives falls into our laps because of the paths we take and the decisions made. You have to have confidence to achieve these things. If you never have a high level of self-esteem, you may never go and ask somebody out on a date that eventually becomes your spouse. You might not have the confidence to make it through that job interview. You wouldn't have the courage to go outside and walk around in the morning. Confidence isn't necessarily natural to our biology, but our need for self-esteem is.

It is important as a parent, teacher, or caregiver to know that while a level of confidence might not be natural, the ability to increase these thoughts and feelings is something we are all capable of. Just because you don't have confidence doesn't mean your child can't.

However, in this process and on your journey through life as a parent raising confident kids, you will want to work on your own level of self-esteem. Children learn by example; you can teach them things through words; but what will be most effective is what they pick up through your actions.

What Confidence Looks Like

Confidence can have a bad reputation. Parents sometimes think that if you are confident, it means you're big-headed. If you are too sure of yourself, you might be egotistical. Those who love themselves are labeled as narcissists.

There is a balance between having high and low self-esteem. You want to be somewhere in the middle. If your self-esteem is too high, you might be blind to some of your flaws. You might believe that you're a perfect person who doesn't need to change, and the other people are wrong when they criticize you.

Confidence that is too low means that you will not have the ability to trust your thoughts and feelings. It means that you won't take the initiative or have the motivation needed to get the things you want and deserve. This is also true for children. Real confidence is not bad. Find an actual happy medium between the extremes of cluelessness and hyper-awareness to achieve a neurotic state of consciousness. There are other misconceptions about confidence that we need to understand. The first is that those who are confident are completely lacking nerves. That is not the case.

Those who are confident are highly aware of the things that make them nervous. They know their anxiety triggers, and they're aware of what they need to improve on. They can recognize bad situations and know how to turn them into something useful. True confidence means that you don't let these things control your actions. True confidence doesn't mean you are not afraid; it just means that your bravery is outweighing any scared thoughts and feelings you have.

Confidence also has a misconception around the image of what that confident person looks like. We associate the loudest person in the room with being the most confident. You might think that confidence means being brave to wear whatever you want and say whatever is on your mind. That's not true either. Confidence is something we all experience on different levels. You can stay silent and not say a single word while still exuding confidence. You can make mistakes and mess up while boosting your self-esteem in the process. There is no one singular way to be confident. We have to recognize this so we can begin to teach our children.

A confident child isn't necessarily one who is going to be some actor running up on stage. It's not always about how comfortable they feel around others or the way they show their fearlessness. Confidence is felt first on the inside. Confidence for children means they will trust and believe in themselves. They will be aware of the things they have to improve on and will continually fight for a growth mindset. Those who are confident don't need other people to reassure them. Validation comes from within rather than external sources. Confidence means they can accept both criticism and compliments from other people. They'll recognize when they are good or bad, smart, or clueless, and so on. They will not be afraid to speak up and ask questions. They're going to be exploring and discovering things without the fear of being judged along the way.

Confident individuals are happy for others; they celebrate their success and are continually looking to change and grow. They won't be afraid to admit that they're wrong because it means they will learn something new along the way. Confidence is good and is not something to fear.

It doesn't mean that you have a huge ego or are a blind narcissist who can't recognize their flaws. This is something we need so we can best teach our children how to exude self-assurance.

The Benefits of Self-Esteem

There are actually a plethora or a myriad of advantages to having a positive self-image. Having high self-esteem means you are assured of yourself. When you can grow this in your children, they will be confident that they are capable of anything. They will have faith in the person they are. They recognize the good feelings existing inside of themselves, and they can find their purpose. They create their own values and have a healthy vision what they want in this life. They have established goals for their future, and they will do everything in their power to achieve them.

Children with high self-esteem will be able to stand up for the things they believe in. They embrace the challenge and are afraid of the uncertainties that lie ahead. They will not look to other people for approval, and they recognize that it's okay not to have all the answers. They won't be afraid, and they'll be more in control of their emotional state. You want to elicit these feelings in your children to ensure they are turning into happy and healthy individuals.

Aside from the fact confidence is essential for everyone, we have to look at critical reasons for why self-esteem is vital for children. They have to learn that despite any shortcomings or mistakes, they are still valuable people who deserve love, respect, and kindness from others. If you are not adequately giving these kinds of validations to your child, they will not be able to take the steps necessary to live a happy and fulfilling life.

The most important thing we want for our children is to give them the life they deserve where they are constantly feeling good about themselves and proud. When we begin to take that away from our children, it causes issues with the way they view themselves.

As children get older, they will only encounter more difficult problems. Before you know it, your kids will be in high school, where they might be subject to bullying or increased social pressure. These times present a heavier risk of depression or even suicide if children don't have self-esteem to assure them. They are deserving of love and worthy of compassion.

Children not only need to have confidence so they treat themselves kindly but it should extend to others around them. You don't want your child to be the bully because they have such low self-esteem to build it up. You don't want your kid to get in fights or struggle with relationships later in life.

If we don't give our children proper self-esteem when young, it will only continue to negatively impact them well into their adulthood. When you fail to provide the fundamentals for strong self-esteem, you are placing them at risk for academic and interpersonal difficulties, battles with mental illness, and the use of risky coping techniques such as drugs or alcohol.

When your kids are confident, they will work through their problems better. There will be less fighting and they will be more respectful and less likely to act out just to get that extra attention. They will believe in themselves and know their worth, able to make their own decisions. They can become independent and successful adults when we provide them with the resources needed to create the right perspectives and feelings.

Chapter 9
How to Understand your Child Has Low Self-Esteem When

Stacy was excited to take her little boy to daycare. He was an only child and didn't have a lot of children to play with. But today, he would have a chance to make some new friends. Stacy was excited. If this experience went well, she planned to make this a regular thing. She went to extensive lengths for the perfect daycare, where her little boy would not only get the care he needed but one with tons of toys as well. The kids seemed friendly, and their caregivers were professional and happy.

The first few days seemed okay, and Stacy thought everything was going well. She was finally settled and could go back to work in peace. Then she started to notice a few changes. Her son was always excited to come home and seemed to brighten whenever the parents were around. When asked about his day, he would respond that it was fine, but he would never get into details.

Stacy did not read much into it. She thought maybe he needed a little more time to adapt to the new environment. When she went back to work, she forgot about her son's issues for a little while. She became engrossed in running her department and integrating back into work so her family had to take a back seat. At least for a while. She would occasionally ask her little boy about his day, but the answer was always the same. "It was okay. I played with my truck."

Things did not change when he went to kindergarten. He seemed excited to join but soon went back into his cocoon. Stacy went to school to ask his teacher about it, but nothing seemed to be a miss. He was just one of the "quiet ones". When her son started complaining a lot, something in Stacy told her that something was wrong. Maybe he needed some help. But when the tantrums became apparent, she was forced to be a little tough on him. "You can't have it your way all the time," she would constantly tell him.

One day at dinner, her husband asked a question that made Stacy look at the situation from a different angle. "Who are your friends at school, Tom?" Stacy looked at her son, eager to finally hear him talk about his schoolmates. But her little boy took a while to answer, thinking hard. When he finally did answer, his eyes never left his food, his voice was low, and his hands fidgety.

"I don't know. I don't have friends."

"So who do you play with?"

"My toys mostly. Or I draw."

"I'm sure you must have someone you talk to," she prodded.

Pause.

"Not really. I guess they never want to play with me because I don't know the games."

"What if you learned how to play? It would be fun to learn something new, right?" She tried again, looking at her husband to contribute. He watched, probably too stunned to know what to say.

"There is no use. They won't teach me."

Another long pause. Stacy did not know how to respond. She could feel the pain her child was going through, and at the moment, she was helpless. Anything she said after this would probably not help the situation. She looked at her husband pleading with her eyes for help.

"Tell you what, buddy, why don't I teach you some games over the weekend?"

"Sure."

Stacy and her husband looked at each other. Their once excited, full of life boy was now timid and shy. She did not understand this. When did this happen? Stacy noticed that Tom had lost weight, and he had barely touched his food that evening. She instantly became worried and lost her own appetite. How was she going to help?

Confidence in kids is the same as confidence in an adult. It's how a person views themselves and what they believe to be true, even if it isn't. A child with a healthy self-view develops into a healthy confident adult - what we all want for our kids. The confidence and self-worth of your child will change at different stages in his/her development, and most parents depend on physical things to notice the change.

You notice their verbal and non-verbal skills, maintaining eye contact, eating habits, among others. Like Stacy's case, monitoring your child's self-esteem is not always a great concern unless you notice something is terribly wrong. Your child will have gone through a lot of wounds, tried to communicate their dissatisfaction in life and their feelings of inadequacy, but somehow, you will miss them.

This is usually because parents don't know what to look out for. When kids are young, it's not easy to notice when their self-esteem is suffering. It's more noticeable when they start school when self-confidence becomes more apparent. Noticing a lack of confidence when your child is younger, however, prevents more serious issues when they are older. There are several ways to know if your child is suffering.

Direct Manifestation

Shame

With some kids, it's easy to tell when they are weighed down, often in how they talk about themselves. Listen to your child and watch out for words such as "I'm stupid, I can't make any friends, I'll never get it done, I can't do it, there is no point in trying," and tons of other phrases like these. Your child will be in despair, seem sad, or lose hope. Their faces will be dim, and their shoulders and head will be down.

In Stacy's case, her son's behavior coupled with how he spoke about having friends was a clear sign of low self-esteem. Stacy does not need anyone to spell it out for her. When talking about friends, Tom's shoulders and head were down, he avoided eye contact, and his voice was low and timid - a sign of shame. Kids who feel shameful adapt postures that make them feel small.

Pessimism and exaggeration

It's often difficult for your child to enjoy anything else if they don't feel good about themselves. For instance, your child will usually predict a negative outcome to situations when you and others view it very differently. The glass will always be half empty in their eyes. In some cases, kids tend to exaggerate the situation in a bid for sympathy and attention. It works for a while, but eventually, it fails and only makes them feel worse.

Blame games

We all want to believe that it's not our fault the way we feel, The same goes for kids. They will either sink into the extreme of blaming themselves and feeling helpless, believing that nothing can be done, or blaming others. "If only this would change then things would get better" is their motto. The problem is that deep down they know it's not true, and eventually, it leads to shame.

Using Coping Strategies to Mask Low Self-Esteem

Kids like Tom can easily express their low self-esteem, but it's not always the same for all children. Some, especially teens, will mask it by adopting coping mechanisms. It becomes difficult for parents to know something is wrong unless they take a keen, close look. This is seen in kids with learning difficulties. These kids believe that their failures and mistakes are out of their control, and they develop what psychologists refer to as "learned helplessness." Their image of the future is filled with failure, and they cannot see light at the end of the tunnel.

Kids and adults naturally develop coping mechanisms to help them manage everyday stresses and changes. But there is a significant difference between kids with high self-esteem and those with low esteem. Kids with high self-esteem will develop mechanisms that are adaptive and lead to self-mastery and growth. For instance, they will get a math tutor if they are having problems. A child with low self-esteem will adopt coping mechanisms.

Quitting

Kids become easily frustrated when they can't succeed at a task, and then they quit. Once they quit, they offer excuses and avoid doing the task altogether. Ever heard your child say, "it's dumb or it's boring?" That's a sign of quitting.

Avoiding and clowning

This behavior is a close relative of quitting. The difference is in avoiding: the child does not want to start the task altogether. In quitting, they will have started and abandoned the task in the middle as they fear lurking doom. Kids often start to make jokes and act silly when they feel pressured to do something. This is called clowning.

Controlling

A lot of kids often become controlling and try to tell everyone else what to do to mask their feelings of inadequacy. For example, they will want their classmates to play the games they choose. If they don't comply, the child will abandon the game and refuse to join the others.

Aggressiveness and bullying

When they feel vulnerable, kids tend to bully others to mask their feelings. They spot victims who show certain weaknesses, often the ones they suffer from, and make them feel worse about it.

Impulsiveness and denying

Being impulsive is often a child's particular temperament, but kids with low self-esteem use it to mask their true feelings. For instance, kids will finish their work quickly, even when it's not well done so they can get out of a task they don't like. Kids will mask their insecurities by denying they are worried about something.

Chapter 10
How Do You Actually Build a Better Relationship with Your Child?

The American Psychological Association says that a good kid's growth depends on a strong bond between parent and child (Kalpana M). The PCR needs parents that are sensitive, dependable, and caring to do well. Tips on how to strengthen the relationship are as outlined below:

Start from the Roots

The mother-child bond is formed in the womb, but the father-child bond is formed as soon as the infant is born. Studies show that father-child relationships are stronger when father involvement begins early on.

Involve Yourself

When it comes to showing your children how much you love them, quality time and effort are crucial. In contrast to the necessity for parental involvement and connection in the lives of younger children, teenagers require a certain amount of seclusion.

Focus on the Child's Well-being First and Foremost

You must put the needs of your children first. If you want to show your child that you care about them, spend as much time as possible with them.

Make Yourself Accessible

Consider the actual physical and emotional requirements of your child. To be a caring and attentive parent, you must be able to see things from the child's perspective. To better understand their feelings, encourage your children to talk about them. Allow them to express their feelings in a non-judgmental way. If you are a first-time parent, this may be difficult, but with practice, you will become more adept. Understanding your child's point of view can make you realize why they're acting out in a particular way.

Talk, Talk, and Talk!

Communication between you and your child must be honest, powerful, and friendly to be successful. Do not be afraid to lay out the ground rules. Keep in mind that a child will try to jangle your nerves. Parental responsibility requires you to be mature and calm in your response.

Consider their academics, friends, and activities: involved parents have great relationships with their children. Find out what's going on in their lives, what they're studying, and who their pals are. If you have spare time, keep in touch with your child's teachers or consider volunteering at the school your child attends. If you're listening to your toddler while working and only answering with a "huh" or "okay" in between, you're not paying attention. Stop what you're doing and pay attention to your child when they talk to you. While conversing with them, make sure to keep your gaze fixed on them.

Make Time with Your Family a Priority

Spend time together at mealtimes and share the day's events. Attending movies, concerts, and other live events should become a regular occurrence in your life.

To have a strong relationship with your child, you must have faith in him or her and be trustworthy. For your child to feel safe and secure, he or she needs to trust you completely. By maintaining your commitments, respecting their individuality, and keeping their confidence, you earn their trust. However, you should not naively put your faith in your youngster and instead do regular inspections. To improve your child's self-confidence and self-esteem, constantly encourage and motivate him or her. Criticizing or correcting someone regularly can make them feel they aren't important.

Respect Your Child

Value their uniqueness and respect their convictions. While you play a role in the formation of your thoughts and attitudes, many other circumstances play well. So that they'll respect you, treat them with respect. Your relationship with your child is strengthened by the love and attention you provide. However, a bad PCR can be caused by certain behavioral issues.

Chapter 11
Typical Parenting Mistakes that Affect Children's Self-Esteem

The goal of any parent is to raise their children's self-confidence and self-esteem. Some of the things that parents do with good intentions, according to the newest study, may really be harmful. This is especially true since our behaviors might drive our children to question our sincerity and cause them to be fearful of failing.

Here are the six most typical errors that parents make, generally caused by a lack of understanding of the ramifications of their actions:

Using Evaluative Praise

Developing a child's self-esteem begins with making them feel good about themselves, and many parents believe that the most effective method is to shower them with praise and encouragement on a regular basis. And although it is true that certain kinds of praise and encouraging remarks spoken to our children are likely to inspire them, research has shown that some praise might do more damage than good in certain situations.

Studies have found that giving children positive reinforcement with statements such as "You're smart" or "I think you're good at this" can increase their fear of failing because they are afraid of doing anything that might expose their "flaws" or call into question their "talent". Despite this, praise is often employed by parents since it was recommended by parenting experts during the "self-esteem boosting culture" of the past couple of decades.

Using evaluative language concentrates attention on our children's innate qualities rather than their capacity to learn new skills, and we run the danger of forcing them to conform to a certain identity. When children identify as "smart" or "good," they may feel under pressure to live up to that impression all the time, and this pressure may drive youngsters to become fearful of failing.

As a consequence of this pressure, children become reluctant to attempt new things or take chances for fear of not "doing it right"; and as a result, they lose out on important opportunities to build their confidence and sense of self. They are also more inclined to dismiss their parents' expressions of affection as they become cynical and begin to question their authenticity.

Instead of helping youngsters feel better about themselves, evaluative praise often has the reverse impact, causing them to become more self-conscious and concentrate on their flaws. "How can I be an exceptional reader?" may be a child's response if we tell them they are good readers, for example. "It really took me twice as long to complete the book as it did for the rest of the actual students in my class." Additionally, it might elicit sentiments of quick denial and skepticism, such as, "I don't understand why they're complimenting my artwork when the one I made yesterday was so much better - they're simply saying this to make me feel good." Sometimes, it might be seen as manipulation: "I haven't done anything to earn their praise; they must just be saying it because they want something from me."

Evaluative praise, even if given with the best of intentions, places an undue amount of pressure on children to live up to our idealized picture of their abilities and talents, and it often results in youngsters feeling uncomfortable. Indeed, many parents have discovered that the more praise they offer their children as they get older, the more quickly their children reject it! To be clear, this does not imply that parents should refrain from praising their children; in fact, the reverse is true.

Focusing on the Outcome

If we focus on the outcomes of our children's activities and exams, praising them with statements such as "I'm so proud of you for getting 100 percent on your school test," we may inadvertently overlook the effort our children have put in on those occasions when they do not excel or are not successful, which can be detrimental.

Furthermore, solely praising our children's successes risks establishing the attitude that they must always "win" or be successful, and that failure to do so is at hand. This feeling may cause some children to be afraid of new tasks. Fearing they would fail us if they do not do them properly, they seek to avoid situations and difficulties that may show their incapacity.

It may also lead to believing that if they do not achieve the intended result (such as the scoring well on a test or winning a football game), they would not obtain their parent's approval. And for many youngsters, this seeming withholding of praise might be seen as a kind of criticism by their peers.

Criticizing and Comparing to Others

The regular "diet" of corrective feedback or "constructive criticism" that a youngster receives is the most demotivating thing that a parent can do for their child. These individuals may feel singled out as if they are being humiliated for features of their personality or behavior.

In spite of this, it is very easy for parents to get in a state of "error detection" or "fault seeking," especially when they believe their kid is being lazy or not putting forth enough effort. This is especially true when it comes to tests and grades. It is tempting to look at a test and point out all of the errors, which is especially demotivating for youngsters who are already struggling.

When we concentrate on praising the child's accomplishments rather than flaws, it helps to build their confidence and think they are competent and able to develop in the future. In the event that we are required to offer feedback, it is critical that we do it in a manner that will not undermine their trust. Furthermore, it is critical to avoid making comparisons between them and a better-behaved sibling or school buddy since this is demotivating and may carry the message that they have inherent problems and as a result have little or no potential to improve.

Overpraising and Going Overboard

The practice of constantly praising children for even the smallest of accomplishments may seem to be a positive means of strengthening their confidence, assisting them in becoming more capable and improving their behavior. In fact, many parenting gurus still advocate for this form of ongoing "positive reinforcement" in their discussions with clients. However, according to studies, praising youngsters without regard to their abilities implies that our praise is more likely to be meaningless and to lose its ability to impact them over time.

By constantly receiving positive reinforcement, youngsters are more prone to develop a "praise addiction" and become too affected by what other people think of them since they are used to being assessed. Additionally, it increases the likelihood that kids would develop into "people-pleasers" in their adult lives and seek continual approval. Consequently, individuals may find themselves constantly being either "made" or "broken" by the opinions of others.

If we get too enthusiastic while congratulating children for even the most little accomplishments, this might cause them to question our sincerity. In other words, if we praise our children excessively, we may discover that they grow cynical about our praise and begin to distrust the sincerity with which we express our affection for them in the long run. Children are really adept at recognizing when we are not being genuine in our interactions with them, and if we do this too often, we may discover that it begins to have a detrimental effect on the trust and connection we have with them.

In particular, this is true of older adolescents. Although younger children prefer to believe what we say without inquiry, teens are typically more aware of the probable motivations underlying our words and behavior. Maintaining a healthy degree of skepticism as well as the capacity to question comes with growing up, so keep this in mind while complimenting your older kid.

Using Reward Systems and Sticker Charts

In recent years, reward and sticker chart systems have been very popular among parents, who use them to promote their children's excellent behavior while also assisting them in developing a positive attitude toward daily work and domestic responsibilities.

However, although such methods may be beneficial short term, the reward chart system teaches children that the main reason for being well-behaved is to be paid. Research has shown that the external incentive offered by the reward grows greater than the internal drive provided by merely doing the task in the manner expected of them. This implies that if we frequently praise and reward our children for anything they do today, we are essentially decreasing the likelihood that they will repeat that behavior in the future unless they are cajoled with further incentives.

Because incentives and sticker charts often provide immediate and stunning outcomes, some parents find it difficult to accept this as a reality. The shift in behavior, on the other hand, is unlikely to remain since such incentive systems are solely concerned with enhancing the outward motivation of the youngster, rather than having any significant impact on their beliefs or attitudes. This is due to the very fact that incentives do not inspire children to reflect on or accept responsibility for their actions, do not aid in the teaching of "right from wrong:, and do not have any impact on their moral development. Rather, they serve to reinforce negative behavior.

They are simply a method of bribing children into doing what we want them to do; and once the reward is removed, the good behavior fades. On a long-term basis, parents are likely to discover that their children come to expect increasingly greater rewards, to the point where by the time they reach the age of teenagers, they may refuse to comply with any of our requests unless they receive some form of reward, such as a financial incentive.

Focusing on your Feelings rather than your Children's

We all want to tell our children when they achieve something that we are pleased with them. For example, "I'm very proud of you!" and "You've truly impressed me" are two of the most frequent expressions that parents use to express their pride in their children's accomplishments. Despite the fact that such expressions are benign and well-intentioned, they are nonetheless appraisals of a child's activities, and they place the emphasis on what adults think about the circumstance rather than on the child's own self-evaluation.

It's also possible that children may understand such words as indicating that it's more essential to please their parents and make them proud of them than it is to just participate in an activity for the purpose of learning, growing, and developing personally.

You do most of the above? Do not despair!

If you're used to making some or all of the mistakes listed above, which is very common, do not despair. This book's objective is to equip you with more effective ways of praising that help raise your child's level of self-esteem and maximize their chances of growing to become confident and independent adults.

Chapter 12
Your Contribution to Your Child's Confidence

The Gift of Consequences

When you step in and do things for your child that he or she could have figured out how alone, you take away the opportunity to become more capable. Remember, feeling capable is what self-confidence is all about, so allowing your child to become more skillful will automatically improve self-confidence.

Sometimes in our rushed days, it is easier to do things for our children that they could do by themselves. Also, when our children become very frustrated, we feel compelled to ease their pain. In both cases, this robs our children of the gift of consequences that could have increased their confidence level significantly.

Becoming patient and allowing more time in the schedule should work out well. For example, if your child is learning how to pack a lunch and get homework ready for school without your intervention, you may need to wake up a few minutes earlier to provide an ample amount of time.

Giving your child the opportunity to fail and learn to do things on his or her own does not mean you stop doing everything for them. As a cheerleader, you are always on hand to offer positive instructions and suggestions, yet only if your child is definitely stuck and not just because you are in a hurry or want to save them from feeling frustrated.

The Cost of Words

Words tear down or build up confidence, and the words you use with your child will become very important to keep in consideration. While you want to be a positive cheerleader, you do not want to pretend that everything is perfect all the time or your child will not grow.

Refraining from being too critical of your child is important. At the same time, you can always talk about making improvements if needed. It helps if you approach this discussion by asking questions. Examples of questions to talk about making improvements could be, "What do you think about trying it this way...?" or "I noticed you remembered to do your homework, would you be able to add this to make it better?" are some ways to talk about making corrections while still building self-confidence. Helping your child through failures is a crucial time for using the right words to increase self-confidence. If you use words such as "You just are not cut out for that..." or other discouraging words, you will ruin the confidence your child has.

On the other hand, if you use words of encouragement, such as "I am so proud of you for trying!" or "You can do anything you want if you keep working hard at it, let's find out how to do that..." they will become words of gold to help your child's confidence levels soar.

Getting to Know Your Child

Getting to know your child's strong points and passions will help you guide them to excel in what they are best suited for. When a child can shine at activities that he or she is especially talented in, that is prime breeding ground to develop ultimate self confidence in every other aspect of life. While you may have high hopes that your son or daughter will be a great sports star or be able to play piano, neither of these may be the best pursuits for him or her. You may have to let go of some of your expectations which will give your child freedom to follow what they are passionate about.

Knowing your child instead of expecting them to be someone you want them to be will allow you to capitalize on their strengths and fortify their weaknesses. It helps to provide an abundant supply of experiences in order to help your child learn what they really love. When your child shows a strong interest in something, encourage him or her to pursue it even if it is not what you had in mind. You never know: your child just may surprise you by becoming excellent at something you never dreamed of. The self confidence that increases because of this is deeply significant.

Boosting Problem Areas

Everyone has qualities that can decrease self-confidence if not handled in a healthy manner. Physical appearance and intelligence are two areas that can create challenges if a person thinks they do not live up to society's ideals. If your child struggles to feel accepted, it will be difficult to increase his or her self-confidence. The best thing you can actually do as a parent is avoid saying things such as "It is stupid to feel that way" if your child complains about being ugly or not smart enough. Instead, you say, "I am sorry you feel that way" and then start to make resolutions.

For a child that feels ugly, getting a haircut or talking about how everyone feels ugly sometimes can help. If he or she struggles to learn, finding help to keep up with friends is an important undertaking. Additionally, continue to point out the positives. Talking to your child about how everyone has likes and dislikes about themselves is important. Then letting him or her know it is perfectly okay to not be perfect in every single way will help a great deal.

CHAPTER 13
RECOGNIZE YOUR SUCCESS AND FEARS

Recognizing your child's anxieties as well as their accomplishments is critical in assisting your them in developing a healthy degree of self-confidence. This is especially true when a child overcomes his or her fear to achieve a goal. It's crucial to remember that when trying to boost a child's self-esteem, every small victory should be celebrated. Your youngster will gain significantly from you acknowledging their accomplishment, no matter how minor the task.

This section of the book will provide you with some useful information to help you recognize your child's accomplishments and worries. It will a serve as your guide, so pay close attention and make sure you remember everything: it will undoubtedly assist your youngster in becoming a self-assured individual.

Recognize their Accomplishments and Empathize with their Fears

When it comes to establishing confidence in a child, it is critical for a parent to understand that both are equally vital. First, we'll discuss the necessity of praising a child's accomplishments and how to do so.

Acknowledge Their Achievements:

Praising your child's accomplishments, no matter how insignificant they may appear to you, is critical in the development of confidence. This will make your child feel good about themselves and build their self-confidence because they will feel like they are continually impressing you.

Praising your child's accomplishments rather than continuously pointing out the negative things your child does can really have a favorable consequence. This is understakable because constantly pointing out a child's mistakes makes them feel as though they can't do anything properly. On the other side, always praising your child's accomplishments and refusing to talk to them about their failures will also have detrimental consequences. The child will believe there is nothing they can do wrong. It's critical to strike a healthy balance between pointing out errors and appreciating accomplishments.

When celebrating your child's accomplishments, be careful not to spoil or overindulge them. If you give your child a high reward every time they finish a tiny activity, they will automatically assume this will happen every time they complete something. When the rewards stop, the youngster will be perplexed as to why they no longer receive a reward for a given task, leading to undesirable behaviors. It is suggested that prizes be saved for more significant achievements. When it comes to modest accomplishments, a pat on the back or a verbal compliment will suffice.

Recognize Your Child's Fears

Understanding your child's concerns is equally important for his or her self-confidence. You might be wondering how fear can help a child become more self-assured. The answer is that overcoming fear can significantly increase self-confidence. It is critical to first comprehend your concerns before attempting to overcome them. You don't want to put your child in a position where he or she will fail. Some of the things they are afraid to do may be too difficult for them to handle. Putting a youngster in a situation where they will not win is one of the worst things you can do while trying to increase their confidence. You should speak with your child to find out what they are frightened of undertaking, and then decide whether it is a good idea to encourage them to face their concerns.

Once you have a good understanding of your child's concerns and the potential harmful and positive effects of confronting them, you decide whether or not to encourage your child. One of the very effective methods to boost a child's self-confidence is to complete an activity they felt they would fail because this procedure demonstrates to children that if they set their minds to it, they can do anything, no matter how difficult or frightening.

It's critical not to force your youngster to confront many of their concerns. If you push your child too hard, he or she may have an undesirable outcome. It may cause anxiety in the youngster with long-term consequences. This will damage their self-esteem even more because their fear may prevent them from doing other chores that they are able to complete with ease.

Chapter 14
Unconditional Love

Kids need love – no if's, and's, or but's. They didn't choose to be born to us, so they don't deserve any punishment beyond discipline for an autonomous action. Kids need to be filled with love so they are confident and independent. You may not be a perfect parent at all times, but when you love your child endlessly, it is the most important thing you can ever give them.

Childhood Empathy

It can be hard to show your empathy. Are they crying over a broken toy? Are they sad that they have to go to bed? You might get increasingly frustrated since it can be hard to understand why our children are acting and behaving in a certain way. Empathy is a way to teach them how to be caring and respectful of others. You want to provide them with the knowledge necessary to treat those around them as deserving equals.

While occurring naturally, it can also be taught. Your child will pick up the most about empathy through the way that you treat the individuals around you. They will notice if you are polite to strangers. They will pay attention when you say thank you or "you're welcome" to those helping you. You want to be the biggest role model for your child to learn proper empathy. Empathy is what will help motivate them to have proper social skills. They'll pick up on the thoughts and feelings of others, making it easier for them to function as healthy adults.

To inspire empathy in your child, begin by digging deep into their minds and asking questions when they are sad. Don't just ask them what made them unhappy. Ask them what it feels like, where they are hurting, and why it hurts. Get them thinking about their own emotions, and they'll have the skill of self-reflection develop. They'll be able to manage their painful thoughts and feelings when you are not around.

You are showing them that it is okay to be sad. You are not making them fearful of this emotion. If you try quickly to change that feeling and don't let them be sad or upset, they will think they are not allowed to experience that emotion. Children will `have times when they feel bad whether they are angry, frustrated or just grumpy from being hungry. They might act out in ways that make you upset. It's great to be a happy and positive upbeat parent, but you also want to let your children feel these emotions. It's not as though you have to let them scream and cry and throw tantrums. Simply give them a few minutes to feel the bad things; then, as they start to come down, discuss those feelings. The next tantrum won't be so bad because you're already creating that emotional regulation within.

You can also teach empathy by encouraging the proper way to treat other people. Make sure that they are going out of their way to be helpful and kind to those around them. Give them positive reinforcement and encouraging awards that make helping others worth their while. Let them know that helping people is good for the world. Ask them how they actually feel and why it feels so good to be a caring individual. Talk about the struggles of other people and kids. Read the news together and talk about the things that are a hard to deal with. It might not always be a comfortable subject, but your child needs to learn about the good and the bad as they continue to grow. The more empathy you can display, the more that they will pick up.

You are the biggest teacher for your child as a parent, making it essential to go out of your way to explore their empathetic feelings. It won't make things better just for them, but for you in general.

How to Stop Shaming

First of all, never shame a child. As beings who enjoy social interaction, a personal level of shame comes naturally. For example, your child might pick their nose one day in class, and the other children notice, laugh, and point, alerting them that picking your nose in public is not socially acceptable behavior. They will no longer touch their nose in front of other children, knowing this will cast judgment.

Imagine the way that you might make a loud noise when in a quiet place like a library. The glares from other people can be enough shame to make you more conscious of your movements. The more extreme the shame, the worst that the individual feels. If your child does something simple like spilling milk, you might be quick to yell at them for making a mess. All this does is make the child afraid to mess up. Of course, they didn't mean to spill the milk, and they will be more careful next time, but they will also be terrified and potentially debilitated by the thought of messing up again. Shame is experienced through your reactions when they make a mistake. Shame is also felt during the punishment period after they've done something wrong.

Constructive Criticism

When we discipline our children, it's not about making them feel guilty or bad; you want to teach them right from wrong. As you are teaching them, you want to instill values that influence future behavior. You don't want to connect it to this one instance. Let's say that your child is running around a restaurant and not sitting down as they should. They're disturbing other guests and people are looking, making you feel like a bad parent. The quick reaction might be to grab the child and yell to the point that they are upset and crying. This is normal for many parents, but it's not beneficial for the child. All that is happening is you're casting negativity on them for being active. Running around inside can be inappropriate in certain settings. Let them know when you're trying to calm them down that they should only run around outside. If you have to pick them up and take them there, that's fine! It might seem excessive, but so is yelling at them in public.

Give them a minute to run around and then return to the meal. It might feel like a disturbance to the dinner, but so is a crying child who is outwardly upset. Show them that running around outside is fine, but if you want to stay inside with the rest of the family and eat, then they have to sit down at the table. You're not punishing their activity, just the inappropriateness of the action in that moment. You're showing them that it is okay to be themselves but also to modify their behavior depending upon the setting. The child will learn that you are guiding them. You are showing which situation is proper and which is improper. This serves to create that emotional regulation they need to build confidence within themselves. Then when they are in a different setting and acting a little wild, they can control themselves and question if it's appropriate. They'll ask themselves, "Are we inside, or are we outside?" and they'll discover that since they are inside, they should probably not run around. This creates better behavior, giving them the independence needed to build confidence.

Teaching Over Blaming

Stop making children feel bad for asking questions and acting in a certain way. Stay focused on addressing the core behavior, rather than the specific situation. You are always teaching your children. It's not a system of punishment versus reward. You aren't there to regulate their good and bad behavior; you want to create a mindset where they can monitor themselves. For example, let's say that your child lost their shoe, and you're rushing and trying to get out the door because you're late. The child lost their shoe, so the reaction is to yell at them. You might want to taunt them for always losing things and to be more responsible.

The issue here is that the child needs to learn how to remember more. Making them feel bad about their memory now is only going to create fear and anxiety. It causes their minds to become more frazzled, fostering a bigger delay in the situation. Instead, stop them and calmly talk to them. Ask when they last had their shoes. Tell them to retrace their steps. Take them through the situation, so you're teaching them how to be more aware of the things they are currently losing.

Children are sponges who pick things up from other people, and they're always learning what's appropriate and what's not through social situations. If you shame your child for something they say, they will be afraid to speak up. If they are not confident with the words that they're using, this can end in debilitating actions. They might feel stupid or shameful, causing them to be angry and lash out. Let's say your child says they hate you. This can be very upsetting, especially coming from a little person that we unconditionally love. To adults, hate can be a harsh word. We know about the challenges and terrible things that occur in this world. A child is not aware of it, and they only know that hate is a very intense word. They heard it somewhere and don't see the consequences of such a strong word. If your child says they hate you, you might respond by telling them it's very bad, and what they are saying is untrue. This response also puts shame on them. Instead, stop and ask why they feel that way and what inside made them say it. Do your best to be very calm, and let them know how much it hurts. Share your side of the story and your perspective, rather than telling them they are wrong. They're still learning and will continue to alter the way that they view a word, such as hate.

Not only are they learning through you what is and what is not appropriate to say, but you are also teaching them how to share their emotions. You're showing them that mommy or daddy can calmly talk when they feel hurt, so next time they experience the same thing, they will do their best to speak to you in a calm and collected tone.

Letting Go of Perfection

As an adult, it can be incredibly difficult not to be perfect. We are in control of our children, so we feel the need to be the perfect person in all situations. It's wonderful to strive for greatness, but at the same time, it can create a sense of low self-esteem within both the parent and child.

There are a few things to recognize if you are trying to be a perfectionist parent. The first is that you might criticize yourself for every little thing. Perhaps you're placing blame on yourself for the shortcomings or mistakes of your child. Maybe they're getting bad grades in school, so you continue to blame and shame yourself. Perhaps they aren't as developed as other toddlers and might not be walking or talking yet. Maybe you're always critical of your actions because it reflects in your children. If you're beating yourself up for not doing enough or questioning whether you're making the right decision, this can make you feel stressed out and overwhelmed. This is going to take a toll on you, which can bleed into how you care for your child.

One thing you have to know about yourself is that you are not to be blamed for every little thing that happens in your child's life. It's important to take responsibility, but remember that guilt does not prove that you are a bad person. Guilt just shows how much you care; it's a reminder that you love your children and want what's best for them. Don't shame yourself and think about all the "what if's," or the "could have/should have/would haves" that are possible. Your child is likely happy and healthy, even when they have shortcomings or have made silly mistakes. If you are not aware of the perfectionist qualities you try to put on your children, consider the following:

Do you struggle to watch your child do something on their own?

Is it difficult for you not to monitor and micromanage every task your child undertakes?

Do you find yourself getting upset when your child makes a mistake?

Do you emphasize criticism rather than praising them?

Do you judge yourself based on your child's actions?

Do you put too much emphasis on the small tasks that your children are doing?

If you answered yes to any of the above questions, first consider the severity to determine if you are a perfectionist parent or not. It's normal to have these traits, and if you feel guilty, know that you are not alone. Keep in mind that our child's shortcomings do not define us. First consider the way that you are talking to your child. Try to suspend your opinion and let your child lead in different conversations.

For example, let's say your child brings home a test, and he got an 89%. Depending upon the child, this could either be abnormal or a huge improvement. If they are consistently getting C's, you are very proud of this accomplishment. Maybe they always bring home A marks, so you question if something was wrong, causing them to get such a low grade. Rather than telling them immediately that they did good or bad, first note that 89% is a good grade. Remind them they should be proud of their accomplishments, whether it is lower than their average grade. Ask them how they are feeling. Don't expect them to be ashamed or proud one way or the other. If they give you the test and you say, "Oh wow, what happened I thought you're going to do better than that?" it sets them up for failure, making them feel like there's something wrong with them. Give them a chance to explain and choose your answer based on that. "That's good, how do you feel about that?" Let them decide on their own whether they feel proud or guilty over the grade. Remember that our children are never going to be perfect: they will never be the ideal of what you have for them.

Apologizing to Your Kids

Sometimes adults get the idea that if they show any sign of weakness, their children will not respect them. They believe they have to excuse even bad behavior so they won't lose any authority. This isn't the case and, instead, parents should do their best to show vulnerability, including apologizing for the mistakes they might have made.

We also have to remember to go easy on ourselves as parents. It's expected for you to mess up. Some of the small things might help build character or teach lessons. What's most important when you do make these mistakes is that you own up to them and apologize. Maybe you lose your cool and end up yelling when they do something wrong. Perhaps you put them down, using harmful words. Don't avoid the situation and act as though it's okay. You are portraying an impossible power struggle.

They'll question why it's okay for you to act so negatively and hurtful but not okay for them. They will question the situation beyond just where the authority lies. You also want to make sure you are teaching them that it is okay to admit you are wrong. When you can say, "Sweetie, I'm so sorry. I shouldn't have yelled at you earlier," you're showing that it's healthy to recognize bad behavior and to try and improve on it. If you are avoidant of the situation, it will teach them that this is how they should handle themselves in the outside world.

Chapter 15
How to Look Confident

It is well known that we make important and long-lasting assumptions about people in the first few seconds of seeing them, before we've even spoken. We look at a person's demeanor, how they hold themselves generally. We notice what they're wearing, the style, colors and condition, and whether it fits and suits them. We note how they're standing or sitting, where they're looking, their facial expression, their eyes, hair, hand movements, and the list goes on.

Think about how you look right now. If someone were to meet you at this moment would they think you were confident? What could you do to alter their opinion? How could you give the impression of confidence simply by changing how you look, stand or hold yourself generally? Note it down.

When I do these things I look more confident............

There are several tips I can pass on to you.

Stand upright with your legs firmly planted both on the floor slightly apart and the arms still. Make sure your shoulders are actually relaxed and your head nicely positioned in the middle to look aligned. When you are positioned this way, you feel in tune with yourself. When we take on a certain physiology to look as if we were aligned and in control, because our minds and our bodies are connected, we also get the feeling of being aligned.

You can have a go at the **seated version** because it is useful in the classroom and at work.

Give good **eye contact**. Look people in the eye, not with a glare but in a relaxed way so you don't threaten them but meet their look. When you look away or look down, you do not look confident and instead look vulnerable. You are more likely to be criticized, picked on, and bullied by those who seek out weaker people as prey. Too much eye contact or when too intense can give the opposite impression, yet it can also be used effectively. For example, as a parent you might want to experiment with using eye contact to communicate with your child. Avoid eye contact when they are misbehaving but give good eye contact when all's well and you want to communicate displeasure.

Be still. Fidgeting with busy hand movements distract from what you are saying or doing and gives the impression of being unsure. You can use your hands but do it deliberately to illustrate a point rather than flapping away, especially in front of your face. Touching your hair and face also indicates a lack of confidence. Young people tend to do this quite a bit, but it doesn't have a place in a situation where they want to appear confident such as in a job interview or when meeting adults.

Choice of **clothes.** Like it or not, you are assumed to have made a conscious decision to wear what you have chosen today. What you are wearing tells other people something about you, as does your choice of how much make up you use. While a lot of makeup may be appropriate on a date, it isn't in an interview or at school or work. Choose clothes that fit: gaping tops with your stomach bulging over your trousers simply indicate you are not buying the right size clothes. Clothes need to be fashionable but not suitable for a night club, and the colors should co-ordinate and suit your skin tone and coloring. Decide consciously what look you want for the occasion because it is your choice as to what you communicate to others about yourself. So take control of it. Needless to say, they need to be clean and not smell!

Move slowly. Running about and fidgeting does not inspire confidence. You look out of control. Make your movements deliberate and fluid so you look as if you know what you're doing and where you're going.

Smile. There may be situations where smiling isn't appropriate, but in most situations, a smile will improve rapport and create the impression that you are confident and have self-worth. Your smile will give the person you are with a sense of self-worth as well, so it's mutually beneficial.

Which of these resonates most with you? Are you someone who rushes about? Do you use your hands a lot? Do you just put on the first thing to hand in the morning? All of these things are signs of a lack of confidence. You will communicate confidence and control when you practice these non-verbal cues.

Why would you want to? Because when you communicate confidence to your children and teenagers, they get it. Yes, they learn from you. They learn by example. You can tell them until you get hoarse, you can give them books and articles to read, but when you demonstrate what you want them to learn, they totally get it.

The other reason for using these non-verbal cues is to manage your state. Your state is your mood or state of mind. When we want to be calm, communicate control and manage difficult situations, we can do this in a more resourceful way if we appear to be aligned and in control. Imagine telling off your child from another room with no eye contact as you're rushing about looking for a stray school shoe?! Yes, I know, we all do it but just how effective is it? Next time, use these tips.

Think for a moment about the people you know who you would describe as confident and self-assured? Put a face to the name and body. Now close your eyes and visualize them. Imagine them in front of you. How do they move, and how do they hold themselves.

How many of these boxes do they tick?

Standing / sitting still

Good eye contact

Good choice of clothes

Moving slowly

Smiling

Make a note to yourself if you need to.

In future when I want to show that I am confident I will ....

So there are many non-verbal signs we can use to create the illusion of confidence for those times when we need it; you'll find that when we act as if we are confident, we feel confident inside as well. This can be enhanced by becoming aware of our values. What is important to us? What do we believe in and are we living our lives according to these beliefs? When we are aligned spiritually and mentally, this translates into our bodies so that they too are aligned. Encourage children as they grow up to live according to their beliefs and values. When they are young, these will probably be the same as yours; but as they learn more about the world, meet new people, travel and read, they will develop their own values and beliefs.

Chapter 16
How to Speak Confidently

Generalizations

When you declare that "everybody" or "no one" says or does something, this is unlikely to be the case, and it lowers your credibility; not just of what you're saying at the time but of everything else you say. Similarly words like always and never aren't likely to be true. When we generalize, it invites others to question what we are saying, which isn't a very confident place to be.

When attempting to persuade your teenager to revise for example, telling them that "everyone knows you have to revise" or that "no one else will leave it until the day before" will not hold sway because they will surely tell you of exceptions. You miss out on important learning when you generalize because it will be the one time when something worked, you felt confident and great, giving you a successful strategy. By focusing on all the other times when things didn't go so well just reinforces the losing strategy.

Distortions

This is when we pass on our responsibility for our own emotions by saying things like '"you make me really cross" or '"you've made me very upset". Our emotions are our own choice; however tempting it might be to blame someone else. When we do this, we lose confidence by showing that we can't take this responsibility and need to offload it onto others.

When your child says that someone made them do something, say something or behave in a certain way, ask "how did they do that exactly, how did they make you do that?" Invite them to consider the choices they had. Choices give them flexibility, and flexibility gives them control. Control of the situation is what we seek in building self-esteem.

Mind reading is another form of distortion. Avoid assuming you actually know what someone else is thinking e.g. "I know you'll disagree but...".This is not a confident start to any conversation and puts yourself in a position where rapport will be hard to achieve. You have already mismatched and indicated that this is your preferred way of conversing. Another form of mind reading is predicting the future, e.g. "You'll end up on benefits if you don't work hard at school." Even if you're sure you're right, it is not possible to predict this. It does not look confident to say things you can't know for sure; it's better to own up and phrase it simply as your own opinion or fear.

Deletions

We frequently delete information that our listener needs to make sense of what we're saying. When someone doesn't understand us and we miscommunicate in some way, we get a sense of low self-esteem; yet by ensuring all the information is there, we can overcome this and communicate in confidence. An example would be "that was so much better". We have not explained what "that" was and how it was better - better than what? I've heard teenagers say, "I wish I was more confident." I need to know more. I ask, "in what way confident?", "when?" "where", "with whom?" There is a lot of essential missing information.

Listen to how confident people talk. They express themselves clearly, and you understand what they are saying.

Initiating Conversation

You will also notice that confident people initiate conversation. They go up to someone they don't know and ask them a question. As children get older, their confidence grows and they begin to take some risks in this area. However, when we start this process off much earlier by encouraging young children to ask for things they want rather than anticipating that someone else will help them, they get used to the process. As parents, we tend to do a lot of anticipating, don't we? We know our children and can guess what they want without them having to ask; but gradually, we start to expect this sort of communication from the toddler, and by the time they are at school, they will be quite used to asking for things. Get them to ask where the bathroom is in the doctor's office or at the dentist. Ask where things are in the supermarket and make sure they associate this with confidence by giving them specific feedback such as, "Well done; that was a sign of how confident you're getting now."

Expressing Opinions

Being confident isn't just about being able to converse with people; it's also about expressing yourself and being true to your values and beliefs. This is also true for children and much more so for teenagers who have a well-developed sense of their own identity, which may be different from their parents and peers. Being able to be themselves and not conform to society stereotypes in terms of fashion, body shape, celebrity culture, and so on, all contribute to them becoming "their own person", and this is a sign of confidence.

When your child expresses an opinion that seems to have been thought through and is true to their values, notice and mark it as a sign of confidence. It can be tempting when the opinion differs from yours to argue or find it annoying, but remember it is their opinion. It may change but for the moment this is their belief.

I believe that confidence is about being comfortable in one's own skin. In France they say *bien dans sa peau*, which means the same thing. This is not necessarily about what people say or do but is more a feeling one gets in their company. It is about feeling aligned and at one with the world. This is not usually a constant state, but it's good to recognize it when you have it so you recognize it next time. This is a gift to pass on to your children. When they seem comfortable in their own skin, check it out and make them aware of it so it becomes a desirable state in the future.

I have shared a number of ways to recognize confidence in yourself, others, and your children. I have also explained how to look and sound confident. Remember that you are their model for confidence so when you use signs of confidence yourself, they will follow your lead.

Chapter 17
Self-Esteem Vs Self-Confidence

A lot of people confuse self-esteem and self-confidence. In fact, when people talk about confidence, they're talking about self-esteem and vice versa. It's too easy to think that self-esteem and confidence are the same. No, they're not. They're two entirely different things. They impact you - the one thing they have in common. But they operate different in impact and application. In short, they run on completely different tracks.

It is critical to understand how self-esteem and self-confidence are different while also being related. By knowing how these two concepts play out in your life, you can put together a winning framework that will enable you to live life with greater self-confidence. That is our ultimate goal; but to get there, we still need to address self-esteem.

What is Self-Esteem?

Your sense of self-worth is your assessment of yourself. When you gaze in the mirror, you make all kinds of snap judgements. Your story or personal narrative about your value as a person, your position in the world, and your worth is something you create. Are you someone worth sacrificing for? Are you deserving of anything? How important are you? These are questions of self-esteem - value questions - that put a value on yourself.

What is self-confidence? It is the external projection of the value, place, worth, importance and effectiveness you feel. While self-esteem is entirely internal and plays out in a civil dialogue and personal narrative that few people see, self-confidence is very much public. To put it another way, if you believe you are a total failure, you will begin to behave in ways indicative of someone prone to failure. You begin working as if you are a person of little worth, as if you do not respect yourself or your abilities.

A person's sense of self-confidence is manifested in the signals they provide to the rest of the world about how they understand and regard them. As you may have already guessed, self-confidence and self-esteem are inextricably linked: both stem from the same source. While one is strictly internal, the other is outward and visible to public. This is what causes people to become perplexed. A large number of individuals believe they are the same. Although they originate from the same source, self-esteem is a completely internal phenomenon.

Put another way, you can be mistaken for being a success. People may believe that you are wealthy, powerful, and extraordinary based on external evaluations. However, if you feel you are worthless, no amount of external affirmation will ever be enough to make your low self-esteem go by the wayside. After all, self-esteem is an internal evaluation of your worth that corresponds to a personal story about your position in the world, relevance, and worthiness.

Self-Esteem is Internal Self-Confidence

I don't want to confuse you, but if you're looking for a simple summation of self-esteem, it's this: it's internalized self-confidence. You see your value as a person and believe that you have value. You can do it. You do have what it takes; you do belong, etc.. It's just an internalization of your capacity and the value you choose for yourself. However, it's important to note that self-esteem goes back to private valuation. It's intimate and internalized. When you focus on your value, you focus on your worth.

The External Components of Self-Confidence

If self-esteem is internalized self-confidence, then self-confidence is externalized self-esteem. I don't want to actually confuse you here, but since the base of your personality is what you choose to value in yourself, meaning your self-esteem, then it follows that what you do as far as the world is actually concerned is an emanation or an outward working off of what's going on inside. In other words, it begins with self-esteem and what you choose to believe about yourself. It starts with your narrative regarding your place in the world, your value and importance, and what you're capable of. However, it progresses from there.

What is the objective manifestation of this? What does the world see? Well, the world outside picks up specific clues. It pays attention to your body language. Do you carry yourself in a way such that people feel you are confident about your ability to get things done? Or at the very least, are you satisfied that you know what you're talking about? Does your body language reflect this?

People also pay attention to facial expressions. Do you have a tough time looking people in the eye? Do you always feel you have to look sideways because you are embarrassed? Do you have a tough time giving certain facial expressions? These are interpreted because confident people have certain expressions. They're not out to dominate other people; they're not out to hit people over the head with their confidence. Instead, their self-faith is natural. It puts people at ease, but at the same time, you can tell that this person is stable inside.

Furthermore, self-confidence is manifested in how we handle situations. When something embarrassing happens or can potentially lead to conflict, is it your instinct to immediately run away or say sorry? Does your intuition immediately take fault and just paper things over, and hope people will not see your screw-up? How you handle situations has an impact on how people take you seriously.

If you are a take-charge type of person, people will sit up and pay attention because there are few people like that: most are passive. How you handle situations is directly impacted by your level of self-confidence. Even the words you choose are reflections of how confident you are. Sure people don't say, "I don't have any money. It's impossible." Instead, they use different phrasing, "How can I do that? How can I raise the money?" In other words, they pose a question that at least has some answer and lead to their desired outcome3.

Compare this with dismissive statements, "I don't have the money. I'm broke. It's just not going to happen." Which type of person would you rather hang out with? I thought so. Finally, another external component of self-confidence involves how you speak. If you're a person who can't talk with enough volume to instill confidence in your competence, that's going to be an issue. People are not going to come to you for answers or be inspired. How can you give them what they're looking for when it's obvious you don't even know yourself? Or at least, give signals that you feel what you're saying and believe is right? How important are these external signals of self-confidence? Well, they're significant because they impact others. Remember that when you are self-confident, you're not just self-confident because you have nothing better to do. Self-confidence isn't just some sort of tag, label, or decorative element. It's not like a bright jacket you wear to which people would point and say, "Oh. That's nice." No, it has an effect on those around you builds up to change your role.

Just how does this play out? When you send out external signals of confidence, you impact other people's trust. They become more comfortable and feel more familiar. They are more willing to help. All these lead to higher and higher levels of respect and lead them to think that you're part of their team and there's a connection between you.

In other words, when you are confident, you can change your surroundings and your immediate reality for the better. Self-confidence is vital because the world couldn't care less about your feelings. Seriously, you can feel very powerful, but if it's internal, it doesn't manifest into actions. You're just wasting your time because the world only cares about the things you do.

One way you "do things" is to impact or inspire people enough to do things for you or behave differently. That's how the world judges people. It's all objective; it's all about results. All this talk about feelings, emotions, what could've happened, what should have happened, or what they have intended is rubbish.

None of that matters. All that matters is what you do? How can you change your surroundings? How much of an impact do you have on people around you? In other words, the world looks at human relationships and dynamics in the chain reactions that manifest in actions. This is not theoretical or speculation. It is concrete. Either you did something or you didn't. You either had an impact or you didn't.

That's how vital self-confidence is because on an objective level, it changes your reality. When you have an impact on others, they behave differently, and you can start moving toward a common goal. You can begin communicating with each other in a way that makes specific changes happen. Keep in mind that these changes can be positive or negative. That's not the point. The point is that the world only looks at you based on the results you produce. This can be positive as well as negative results.

Chapter 18
Self-Esteem

It is difficult to build self-esteem. We want our children to feel confident and good about themselves. Studies have shown that telling a child she is the smartest person in class can actually do more harm than good. Undeserved "A"s can be a sign that teachers are encouraging a false sense of self-worth in students. High school graduates who do not have the right grades or diplomas will face difficulties when applying for college or interviewing for jobs.

We should all do our best to raise responsible and confident children. However, it is important that we don't give false belief in their abilities and talents. Ask yourself if your child is telling you something positive. If not, find something encouraging that they can say.

Be positive and not defiant in everything you say. Dr. Phil McGraw said, "It takes a thousand 'attaboys' to erase one 'you're not smart enough, you idiot'." Don't make your child feel inferior. Children long for their parents' approval, often well into adulthood. You can let them know right from the start that you love them unconditionally and show your approval by your words and actions.

Be Supportive of His Dreams

If Joel has his heart set on trying out for Pop Warner football, you'll do him no favor if you remind him that he's the smallest boy in his class or he can't even catch the balls you toss him in the yard. Give as much encouragement as you can, and he may surprise you by being the fastest runner on the team. But if he continually misses plays, don't tell him he's the best player the team ever had. He may believe you and stop trying to improve.

We can't always support everything our kids try, but by encouraging them in activities that could help them realize a talent or skill, we help them learn what they can do well. When they know their strengths (and weaknesses), they feel better about themselves and dare to step out and take risks when tackling the bigger things in life: SATs, college exams, or job interviews.

Help Kids Believe in Themselves

Helping kids believe in themselves means to actively encourage them when they struggle with self-esteem issues. When one of Courtney's ventures or projects isn't going well, and she's ready to give up, encourage her to hang in there and look at it from other angles. Point out other options she might try and reiterate the skill or talent that will help her move forward. Suggest books or other helpful materials that might provide further insight into the problem. Remind her that many things in life require hard work and tenacity, and that giving up won't help her achieve her goals.

Point Out Strengths and Skills

Whenever you see your child do something especially well, be sure to point out that they seem to have a particular aptitude for it. We're not talking about how well they make their bed or set the table, but areas where real skill or talent is involved. If Kyle is carving a model ship and doing a really good job, compliment his precision and steadiness of hand. When Alison sketches a skillful design for redecorating her room, emphasize that she may have a flair for art or design.

Their interests may come and go, but the skills involved are indicators of future hobbies or careers. Kyle may end up being a surgeon and Alison could become an architect! Humans are not equally blessed with talent, skill, strengths and weaknesses. Our kids need to realize that there are just some things they might not do as well as their siblings or friends do.

If Patty loves playing piano, but just can't get the hang of playing smoothly and confidently, help her try different tactics. Perhaps she could change her practice times so she's more alert. Maybe a different teacher could bring out the best in her playing. Or it could be that she plays better when playing music she likes, rather than what she's forced to play. Any of these options might help her overcome a perceived weakness. You may all need to face the fact that she just really doesn't have a talent for piano. If everyone agrees that's the case, allow her to relax and just play for her own entertainment. If she's not worried about being perfect, she'll enjoy it more. Eventually she'll find another interest at which she excels.

Start an "Attaboy/girl" list

Often, our kids don't see the value in what they have achieved. They tend to think they can't do anything well. If your child feels like this, have him sit and write down everything he can think of that he's done well. Offer suggestions when he bogs down. The accomplishments don't have to be lofty —after all, he's a kid! Call this the "attaboy" or "attagirl" list and encourage them to add to it as they experience more successes.

Even younger children can list things such as learned how to tie his shoe, won the class spelling bee, got an "A" on a poem, had his drawing published in the school newsletter, came in first in the footrace in the park, or picked some flowers for the sick little girl in the neighborhood. A teen can write that she passed her driving test on the first try, read fifteen books during the summer break, was elected class president, ran in a 5K, or helped repair a house for a deserving family. Be sure to include volunteer activities, so they can understand that giving to others is as important as getting recognition for their own accomplishments.

It's important they realize that this exercise is to help them feel good about themselves, not to show why you love them. Make sure they actually understand that you love them for themselves, not their accomplishments.

Make a feel-good list

This is a good exercise for anyone, especially a child who may be going through that "I can't do anything right!" or "I'm a dummy" phase. It's different from the "attagirl/boy" list in that the former list chronicles past accomplishments while this one is to create an inventory of current traits, talents, and skills.

If Linda is feeling down in the dumps, sit down and have her make a list of all the good things about herself. This list should focus more on personal or character traits, rather than accomplishments. If she's having trouble coming up with items for her list, feel free to jump in and remind her of things you like about her. Include traits such as her kindness, compassion, neatness, willingness to help, her big smile, the pictures she draws for you, that she does her chores without complaining, etc.

Make a game of it and make sure she comes up with a list of at least 20 items. Be sure that she contributes most of the items so she'll realize some of her own best features. Keep the list and have her look at it; even add to it regularly, especially when she gets into the doldrums again.

Save the mementos

When Laurie gets her name in the school newsletter, or even a real newspaper, cut it out and display it on the refrigerator for a while. Then put it in a scrapbook or an "attagirl" file. Not only will it be physical evidence of your pride in her, but it'll be something she'll look back on and enjoy years later.

A friend's son brought home the school newsletter in which a poem he had written had been published. His dad glanced at it and said, "That's nice, Ray," and laid it aside. Later Ray found it in the trash can and ran sobbing to his room. He felt that what he had done—and was so proud of—was meaningless and worthless in his father's eyes. When the dad realized how he'd hurt Ray, he felt bad and managed to reassure him. But how much better it would actually have been if Dad had spent a few minutes acknowledging Ray's creativity and his initiative in writing the poem and submitting it for publication.

Celebrate!

When Justin graduates from kindergarten, wins the class spelling bee, or gets his Eagle Scout badge, make a celebration of it! Our family usually went out for dinner, or sometimes just dessert in honor of an occasion. But an ice cream cone or a favorite treat at home could be just as special. Whatever you actually decide to do, make sure it's known that it's in the child's honor. And if one child seems to excel more than the others, look for ways to celebrate the achievements of all, so the siblings don't feel left out. Celebrate when they write their name correctly the first time or read a picture book out loud by themselves.

Even though you're celebrating achievements, be sure you also express your pride and love for who they are, not just what they do. Celebrate your own successes as well: Mom got a promotion, Dad was elected club president, or working together as a family, you all finally got the garage clean. Treat yourselves to something special. Any reason to celebrate makes for a fun and happy family.

Teach Good Communication Skills

Encourage Jesse to reply to adults with more than one word and to look others in the eye when speaking to them. But don't embarrass him by prompting him what to say during an attempt at conversation. If your neighbor asks Jesse, "How's school going?" and Jesse says, "Fine," you should let it go for the time being. Later, talk to Jesse and demonstrate how he might have added something like, "I'm good at math, but history is hard for me."

You might use a rubber ball to demonstrate that just as it's no fun to play when you throw a ball to someone and they keep it, it's no fun to ask a question and not get a full reply. They should toss the ball back (offer more information) to make the conversation interesting. And who knows, the neighbor might just have some tips on how to remember history dates! If you teach a child these conversational skills while young, he won't be afraid to ask a teacher why he got a low grade and he'll be less likely to get flustered when he goes for his first job interview. Communication skills build confidence!

Encourage Good Health Habits

A healthy body is a major contributor to a healthy self-esteem. The teen who goes to school in dirty clothes, with unwashed hair and fuzzy teeth, is not likely to have many friends. Begin early to instill good hygiene rituals, so that they become automatic as he grows up.

Kids are going to eat whatever they can get away with, and we often have little control over what they eat when not in our presence—especially teenagers. But we can at least make sure they understand the basic concepts of nutrition and well-balanced meals. Explain how good eating habits will help them to be more alert in school, as well as be stronger and more fit for the sports and other activities they want to pursue. Keeping healthy snacks —rather than chips and sodas— available at home, and preparing well-balanced meals will help instill the importance of healthy eating.

Encourage Problem-Solving

It's often n tempting to jump in and solve all the problems our child is facing, rather than let him work them out for himself. But if we do this too often, he won't learn the problem-solving skills that are so crucial later in life. Rather than offer an immediate solution, allow him some time to think about every angle of a situation. Encourage him to write down pros and cons if it's a tough decision to make. You might offer suggestions on ways to approach the problem, without offering to solve it for him.

If he can come up with an answer himself, he'll feel good about his ability to solve the problem alone. And it'll give him the confidence to tackle more difficult challenges as they arise. The parents' greatest job is to prepare their kids to be adults.

Encourage Journaling

Journaling is actually a great way to work through feelings and concerns. Just getting issues down on paper helps to solidify all the murky thoughts that often seem to flit around with no purpose, and yet weigh heavy on our hearts. Girls tend to like the idea of journaling more than boys. It's easier for them to pour their emotions out onto paper. Some boys think journaling is "sissy," so you may have to change the vocabulary or tactics. In either case, if they don't want to keep an on-going journal, at least provide them with a notebook or let them choose a journal they like and suggest they write out concerns, then list ways they might be able to overcome the problem.

If they don't see it as an assignment to write something in it each day, they'll be more likely to turn to their journal when they need to work out problematic issues. And if they record the positive things that happen on a regular basis, they'll have the added benefit of realizing that the good times generally outweigh the bad. When they recognize how much good is done to and for them, and how much they do for others, they'll feel better about themselves overall.

Chapter 19
Building Self-Esteem in your Child

Be a good role model and open a dialogue

Talk to your kids not only about their attention and learning issues but also about the things you see as challenging for them. Talk about your values and mention how you appreciate your weaknesses. If your working memory is weak, say something like, "I don't remember the items I wrote on the shopping list. Next time I'll take a picture just in case I forget to carry the shopping list."

This teaches your child that you are human and have weaknesses, but you use simple methods and strategies to strengthen them. Encourage your child to come up with their own techniques and strategies to overcome their weaknesses. For instance, show them how merely pronouncing words a little different can help them learn to spell or how organizing books in colors can help make homework fun.

Provide clear feedback, but don't be critical

Sometimes it is hard to communicate to children about the things they have to improve on. However, addressing such topics can help your child's self-esteem development. The main point is to talk about their challenges in a motivational way to help them improve and not make them feel inadequate.

Working hard to achieve a goal leads to developing positive self-esteem. So give your child a particular purpose they can work toward, rather than criticize them. For example, instead of saying, "Why are your clothes always in a mess?" You can say, "Your clothes are scattered all over the house. You can get back to your toys after you pick them up and keep them in your closet."

If they have trouble spelling words, encourage them to read a simple book and spell all the words correctly. By the time they are done with three books, their efforts will have paid off, and their spelling will be much better. Help them read and listen to their spelling. Praise their effort and be patient when they can't seem to get a particular word right.

Help in nurturing a growth mindset

Help your child to reframe negative statements and thoughts. Children with a growth mindset are confident they can improve their abilities over time. However, children with a fixed mindset believe their abilities can't change and are set no matter how much they try. For instance, your child may say, "I have dyslexia, so I can't read this because it is too hard." You may respond by saying, "Yes, the reading may be hard for you; for this reason, you may not be able to read the book yet, but we can formulate a plan to help you read it better."

Kids need to learn to take initiative and the solve problems they face, and the first step is always through your encouragement. They will have the courage to face challenges by themselves. Tori's son was fond of complaining about how bored he was in the afternoon. When Tori noticed how much he loved to paint and color, she started to commend his effort and show interest in what he was doing. When he would come complaining about being bored, Tori would tell him to figure something out. He was creative, and she was sure he could come up with something to keep himself busy while she worked. Within a few weeks, Tori had a wall full of painted pictures, improvised toys, and other crafts that her son worked on to keep himself busy. After joining an art class, a way of keeping busy, art turned into a passion. Her son now is a teen and sells his paintings online to earn his allowance.

Making mistakes is a learning experience

Part of possessing a growth mindset is knowing that making mistakes is a learning opportunity. When your child understands that failing is okay and there is a solution to errors, it helps build self-esteem. You may say, "Yes, you poured the juice. Next time you are pouring the juice, hold the glass over the sink."

Another excellent way to show that mistakes are a learning process is to apologize to your kids when you wrong them. Promise them that the error will never happen again and keep your word. Also, look for opportunities to openly admit you are wrong and do whatever you can to make things better.

Praise your child's efforts and approach not only the result

As much as praising your child is important, it matters how you do it. Instead of looking at the result, praise your child on every step he or she took along the way. By appreciating the child's approach, they enjoy tackling the challenges. You help them understand that they can overcome obstacles. Honest specific praise is vital in building positive self-esteem. For instance, you can find ways of praising your child when they work hard on their school projects or home projects. You may say, "I see how hard you work when practicing that song on the piano. I know it was not easy, but it was a good idea asking the piano teacher some questions and for advice."

Encourage extracurricular mentors or interests

Look for an extracurricular activity your child is good at and enjoys. This can help your child discover his or her strengths as well as make academics less of a struggle. In case your child likes to sing, you can find a choir for them to join. Or if they are interested in sports, discuss how to sign up for a softball league or local soccer team. However, if your child is not interested in any extracurricular activity, consider looking for a mentor in other interests they may have. Connecting your child with someone who is ahead of them can build and inspire confidence in your kid.

Point out successful people with attention and learning issues

Knowing there are successful role models, such as celebrities, entrepreneurs, and athletes with attention and learning problems who have faced the same challenges is a good source of inspiration. For instance, actor Daniel Radcliffe said that the stunt work he did for Harry Potter movies helped him overcome the struggles he has with dyspraxia. Lisa Nichols has dyslexia, but she has written some of the best-sellers today.

Encourage your child to pursue their interests.

A sure way to boost self-esteem in children is by encouraging them to do the tasks they are interested in, then see to it that they do it to completion, no matter the task. It could be beating video games or swimming laps. The point is that they stick to what they start to get a feeling of accomplishment. Help them celebrate every new achievement. It teaches your child to appreciate the effort they put into making it happen and also shows that you can blow your own trumpet. Feel good about your accomplishment, whether you have one cheerleader, hundreds, or none.

Love your child

This may seem obvious, but it is the most valuable thing you can offer to your child. It doesn't matter if you do it imperfectly: always pour out a lot of love. Your child desires to feel loved and accepted, starting with the family, extending to schoolmates, friends, the community, and even sports teams. If you ignore, yell, or make any other parenting mistakes, see to it that you hug your child and say you are sorry while assuring that you love them. Unconditional love creates a strong foundation for self-esteem.

Model positive self-talk and self-love

Before teaching your children to love themselves, you must start by loving you. Model this by praising and rewarding yourself whenever you do well. Whether you get promoted at work, run a marathon, or throw a successful party, always celebrate your success together with your children. Talk about the efforts, skills, and talents required to attain those accomplishments. At the same time, also remind your child of the skills she or he has and how they can use and develop them. Also, model positive body image by openly saying you love how you look or your smiles and curvy shape.

Teach resilience

No one succeeds all the time. There will be failures and setbacks not to mention pain and criticism. Use such handles as learning encounters instead of dwelling on these events as disappointments or failures. The old sayings, try, try, and try again, has virtue, especially when teaching your child not to give up. However, it is crucial to validate your 'skid's feelings instead of saying," Oh, cheer up," or "you should not feel so bad." This helps kids feel comfortable sharing their feelings as well as trusting them. They learn that a setback is a part of life that can be managed.

If your child doesn't perform well on a test, don't show him or her pity or tell them that they will never be good at reading. Instead, talk about the steps they can take to perform better next time. When they succeed, they will feel proud of their accomplishments, which will boost their self-esteem.

Instill adventure and independence

Children with high self-esteem are always ready to try new stuff without fearing failure. With younger kids, you will have to supervise them from the sidelines. You can set up situations where they can do things by themselves but make sure it is a safe situation; however, give them some space. For instance, you can demonstrate how a sandwich is made then allow them to try it alone, without intervening or hovering. Encourage exploration, whether outings and day trips, new hobbies, or vacations with schoolmates or teammates. This will enlarge your child's horizons as well as build their self-esteem and confidence in their ability to manage new situations.

Set rules as well as be consistent

Children feel confident when they are aware of what to expect and who is in charge. Although your child may feel your rules are too strict, he or she will feel confident in what they can or can't do when you have set the standards and enforce them consistently. Every household has different rules; however, they change over time, depending on the age of your child. Whatever the rules of your household are, be specific on what's important in your family. Following and learning rules give the children a great sense of confidence and security. And as your child grows older, he or she may have extra input on responsibilities and rules. However, always remember that you are in control and their parent, not their best friend.

Coach relationship skills

Having confidence in relationships is vital to a kid's self-esteem. A loving parent-child relationship is the first relationship our child forms. It's thus, the most important. But as the social circles of your child begin to expand, you have to show him or her how their actions can affect others, and help them to learn how to maintain their self-esteem when other people's actions affect them. As a parent, it is not actually your place to "mend" every situation; instead teach your child the kindness, compassion, self-assertiveness to manage the highs and lows of relationships.

Other Ways to Build Confidence

Give your child choices

Giving your child choices within a reasonable preselected set of options makes them feel empowered. For instance, you can ask your child to choose between pancakes or eggs for breakfast. Learning how to make choices at a young age her for more complicated decisions she is bound to face when she grows up.

Don't do everything they need

Be patient and allow them to do things by themselves. For instance, it may be easier and faster to dress up your preschooler. However, allowing him or her to do it helps them learn new skills. The more they meet new challenges, the more confident and competent they feel.

Let them know no one is perfect

Explain to your child no one expects them to be perfect. How you react to your kid's disappointments and mistakes colors how they feel and their likelihood of sharing their frustrations and errors with you.

Don't offer or gush insincere praise

Children are masters at noticing baseless compliments or insincere praise. Praise your kid often, but give specific compliments so that your words don't sound hollow. For example, rather than responding to your child's drawing with, "Wow, that is great. You are the best artist all over the world". Try putting it like this, "I like how you have drawn the whole family. You also included details like daddy's beard."

Don't compare your children

Instead of comparing your children, appreciate each one's unique gifts and individuality.

Don't use sarcasm when making a point or call your children names

Never overlook your child's feelings; don't say anything that you might regret in anger. And always keep in mind that you can hate the child's actions without hating the child. Make sure you illustrate to your child the difference.

Spend quality time with your kids

Whether it is going for a bike ride or grabbing a bite, always schedule special time for your kids. If you have more than one, schedule time for each and a time when all of you can be together. This is an excellent opportunity to actually strengthen the bond you share and talk about what is on your child's mind.

Our kids are growing up in tough times. The teen suicide rate is soaring. One out of every three children complains of bullying. Kids are under immense pressure to perform academically. With all these stressors, it's vital to help your child maintain a high sense of self and build confidence and self-worth.

The Six Pillars of Self-esteem

Nathaniel Branden was a psychotherapist and writer interested in researching the vast world of self-esteem. Once you begin to understand them, you will be on the right track toward a better and improved version of yourself. These pillars are based on practices of:

living consciously

developing self-acceptance

improving self-responsibility

improving self-assertiveness

living purposefully

living with personal integrity

Improving self-esteem and building confidence requires making peace with yourself. Now that you know how outside events can have an effect on your self-esteem, it's time to separate who you really are from who you pretend to be. As Branden says, it is all about practice. You don't need to worry, as the guidelines below will lead you.

The Practice of Self-esteem

It's important to understand that one's self-esteem level is linked to the actions an individual takes. If you understand what you're doing wrong but do nothing to rectify your behavior, you will end up in the same place. Practicing and working on the way you see yourself should become a habit. You will also see that relying on words alone will do you no good if you don't actually apply what you've learned to your life and your actions.

Nathaniel Branden suggests an exercise to help you fortify this first pillar of self-esteem. It is called "sentence completion" and requires writing six to ten grammatically correct sentences, starting with a predefined prompt. Just remember that you will need to be quick and write down the first thing that you think of. Once you start analyzing your responses, you'll begin to learn valuable things about yourself. Take a look the following sentences and give the exercise a try right now, by filling in the prompts with your responses:

For me, living consciously signifies...

If I increase my awareness by just 5% percent, today I will achieve...

If I am more careful with how I deal with others, today...

If I become 5% more aware of my insecurities...

If I become 5% more focused on my priorities...

The Practice of Self-acceptance

The second step to increase your self-esteem is to accept who you are. This requires an in-depth analysis of your beliefs, the way you act, and your fears. What seems positive for some can be negative for others. It's completely useless to define yourself according to other people's points of view. It's only by embracing who you really are and accepting not only your good parts, but the bad that will heal your mind and soul.

We live in a world governed by standards. Everyone becomes judgmental at times, even when those positions are justified with nothing more than vague and unclear facts. Only by accepting who you really are can you integrate in a dignified manner. You don't have to be ashamed of your weaknesses. Rather, you need to be able to embrace them and fight to become a better person. Hiding what you really feel may seem like a good solution for the moment; but in the long term, it will only make you feel insecure. Feel free to share your true feelings with others and who you really are. They may share with you in kind, and who knows? Maybe you'll help them to improve their own self-esteem as well.

The Practice of Self-responsibility

Being self-responsible means standing for your actions and choices. Don't be tempted to believe that this means you need to respond to your bad decisions. Self-responsibility means much more than admitting you were wrong at some point in your life. To be more precise, the act of being responsible can be translated to mean being able to face the challenges of life. Sometimes it's going to be hard, especially when you have to deal with a break-up or miss out on the chance of being promoted at work. Still, there's no reason to pose as a victim. Opportunities come and go: this is how life works. If you weren't ready for something that happened at some point in your life, it doesn't mean you cannot achieve it later. Always try to better yourself each day.

This is what self-responsibility truly means. It's all about replacing blame with solutions. It would be a total lie to claim that you can always win or to promote unrealistic algorithms for unlimited success. The truth is that every person faces situations beyond their understanding. Feeling ashamed or guilty is never the answer. What you need to do is take on responsibility for your ideas and defend your point of view. You need to be well-informed.

The Practice of Self-awareness

A major aspect that lowers self-esteem is living other people's life stories. In other words, pretending that you're someone you're not to please others. The root of this problem take the people who face it back to their childhoods, where parents or teachers constantly reprimanded them and asked for perfection. Being genuine and standing for an opinion doesn't mean you're wrong. If you feel you want a different job because you discovered the one you have doesn't give you any sense of accomplishment, it doesn't mean you don't want to work or are lazy.

Self-assertiveness can also be defined as living authentically. Be honest and embrace who you are. Though it may actually seem difficult in the beginning, once you learn to leave all your fears behind, you will begin to discover a new you: the real you. Furthermore, allowing other people to tell you how to live your life and pretending you actually enjoy it may make you feel good in the short term, but you'll become discouraged and sad in the long run. Don't be afraid to act and show others what you're really like. Those who care about you will support your opinions, while those who are against you; well, they don't really matter. These people will only bring you down. You need to actually start surrounding yourself with like-minded people who support you and forget the rest.

The Practice of Living Purposely

The fifth pillar of self-esteem is establishing goals. You can only give a purpose to your life when you've begun to understand what you truly desire and then do everything you can to achieve it. There are two major goals a person can set:

long term: to earn a degree, raise a family, get a good well-paying job, start a business, etc.

short term: to buy furniture for the house, plan a summer holiday, learn something to get a raise, etc.

The effect of establishing goals is to energize your existence. It's easier to face daily life when you know what you want to achieve, not to mention how good you will feel once you achieve the desired goal. Sometimes this is easy, like when you shop for new furniture. However, this goal can be elaborated on as is the case when you plan to start a business. You need to be prepared to face ups and downs, but by no means should you give up when faced with the first obstacle. The goal is to never give up and keep pushing to achieve your goals. Having small "wins" raises self-esteem and enables you to become a more confident person.

There's a very important aspect of goal-setting that needs to be taken into consideration. Living purposefully means establishing your own goals. Your goals need to be things that you truly want to achieve and not what others want you to do. They must be the result of your own ideals and values. Don't be afraid to fight for what you want. This will make you a stronger and more confident person.

The Practice of Personal Integrity

The sixth pillar of self-esteem describes the link between ideas and behavior. A confident person acts according to their values. This means behavior needs to be constant. In order to actually make things easier and help you to discover whether you're acting according to your beliefs, answer the following questions:

Is there a link between your ideas, opinions, guidelines and attitude?

Do you feel your ideas play a major role in the way you act?

If the answer to both questions is maybe or no, you need to work harder on your personal integrity. Avoiding standing up for a cause or idea you believe in, or providing contradictory opinions, may cost you dearly. Sooner or later, people will accuse you of hypocrisy. Don't be afraid to take actions that reflect who you really are. Let others influence your personality only if they come with unquestionable arguments. Remember that having an opinion doesn't mean you're wrong or cannot defend your point of view. You need to actually be truthful to yourself first, being honest about who you really are.

Branden encourages people to live consciously. You need to be responsible for the words you say and the actions you take. Furthermore, it's vital to respect others just as you wish to be respected by them. Possibly the most important piece of advice is that small improvements can actually make a difference. There's no such thing as perfection, and this term should definitely be replaced with harmony.

Chapter 20
Praising Your Child and Self-esteem

For many years, conventional wisdom stated that praising a child at every opportunity boosted their confidence and self-esteem. However, in recent years, new research has shown that the wrong kind of praise and too much undermine a child's confidence. Even worse, unearned or non-specific praise can derail the natural development of perseverance and resilience.

A recent study on how the wrong kind of praise can backfire was conducted at Stanford University. Twenty fifth-graders were given problems that required some effort but were easy to solve, so most of them got them right. Afterward, half the students were told they were smart and praised for their achievement, and the other half was commended for their efforts. After a little while, the children were given the choice of taking more difficult tests or another test like the first one. The children who were praised for their efforts were eager to take on the harder problems. But the ones honored for their achievements shied away or chose to do similar tests, which they knew they would pass.

The researchers concluded that simply telling the children they were smart, awesome, or geniuses was setting them up and keeping them from making mistakes that would undermine their 'smart' image. Moderating praise is easier said than done. All parents want their kids to know how great they are and can do anything they set their minds to. However, there must be a balance between cheering them on and fostering their development. Too much praise can turn a good thing into a bad thing. As a parent, you want to boost your child's confidence without increasing their vanity.

When you tell your kid that you are proud of them, it shouldn't be solely based on their performance. They are set to learn more from failure than when passing or excelling at things.

When to Praise your Child

It is essential to know when to deliver praise and when not to and to understand what form the praise should take. If a kid is praised for doing trivial things with commonplace effort such as, "Wow, way to go, buddy, you woke up early this morning!", your praise will lose its power and meaning. Why work for something you will get regardless of whether you try or not? In this case, your praise simply becomes part of the background noise, something they are used to hearing.

Non-specific praise like saying, "You're awesome!" can also undermine your child's confidence because they have no way of knowing what that means and what makes them awesome. They have nothing to actually compare themselves to, and thus they lack an understanding of what it takes to achieve this awesomeness.

Praise as a Positive Reward and its Role

A reward is defined as a prize or other mark of recognition given in honor of an achievement. It is something earned after effort has been put in. A reward is an incentive that increases a target behavior. Studies have shown that if the target behavior is to decrease, what you think is a reward or punishment. The "You are so smart" and "You are very awesome" forms of praise show that even with positive words, the desired outcome, which shows of intelligence or good behavior, decreases. In this case, the positive affirmations function as punishment.

A reward given too often loses its power and influence to shape behavior. This phenomenon is referred to as satiation. The same thing can happen with praise. It is not unusual for children to tune out approval from a doting parent.

Parental attention and response are an inherent part of intuitive parenting and can serve as powerful rewards in themselves. When your child brings you something she made, don't say how great it looks and tell her she is awesome. Instead, take time to ask her how she made it? What materials did she use? If she had any help and if she is thinking of making something else? Showing genuine interest in her work will encourage her to focus more on the process and not the result. This is called a praise transaction. Everyone, especially kids, loves having someone take an interest in what they are doing and engage with them this way.

Remember that the praise should increase desired behaviors, which in this case is having the child continue being creative and express her creativity positively. What you want in the end is for the child to gain enough confidence to express herself, continue in her innovative ways, and be resilient enough to tackle any obstacles, challenges, or people with different opinions. It is these behaviors and skills, not the empty praise, that will foster your child's self-esteem as they grow up.

Your attention and interest in what your child is doing can remain as a form of praise, even when they fail or make mistakes. These moments provide valuable teaching opportunities to reward resilience and persistence. By encouraging them and praising their efforts, you are empowering them to try again. The continuous engagement shows your child that failure is not the end, and failing does not make them less smart or less impressive in your eyes.

How to Praise Effectively

Matthew, a natural athlete, was widely praised from an early age for his throwing and catching abilities by his parents. Once he was old enough to play with other kids, he realized, for the first time, that he was good—but maybe not the best. In Little League games, he would choke up, unable to catch or throw any ball. He constantly looked back to his parents for encouragement and kept forgetting to keep his eye on the ball. He would get upset if his every effort wasn't met with praise from his coach, even when such accolades didn't help him perform any better. Matthew was a bundle of nerves out in the real world, unlike when he played with his dad in the backyard and he got endless praise.

Be sincere about your praise

As you can see, this is a classic case of how praise, or the wrong kind of praise, affects a child's ability to play. His parents wanted him to know that he was good at baseball but overdid it, which turned Matthew into someone who needed his every action noticed and praised. This kept him from becoming a good baseball player. His parents should have praised his efforts and accomplishments when he learned to catch or throw the ball. With praise, he would have put more effort into practicing, and he would have become better.

Praise specifically

Instead of generalizing everything, state what the child did to earn accolades. It is also important to tell them how you feel about it. For instance, if your son picks up his toys from the floor, say, "I appreciate that you picked up your toys without me having to ask." or "Thank you for helping me keep the house looking neat and clean by picking up your toys." Young children do not need praise all the time. The best thing you can do is highlight what they did well.

You should also avoid praising your child in areas they do not have control over. This can include innate and unalterable abilities such as intelligence, physical attractiveness, athleticism, or artistic gifts. Instead, you should direct your praise to areas they have control over, such as effort, attitude, responsibility, commitment, discipline, focus, decision making, compassion, generosity, respect, love, etc.

You should understand that kids are more likely to actually incorporate the specific praise they hear from their parents into their view of themselves. Matthew knew he was praised for being the best from an early age. So when he interacted with other kids, he quickly realized that even though he was good, he was probably not the best. This affected him as he did not understand why his coach never praised him.

Learn when to praise

Praise your child after an accomplishment or good deed. You don't have to honor your child continually. For instance, if you want your daughter to have completed her homework by a certain time, work out a plan and make a homework schedule. You can then praise her when homework is indeed done on time.

It is possible to reduce the frequency of reinforcement after the behavior has been taught or modified. Once the homework schedule becomes normal, you may gradually reduce the amount of constant praise you provide; nevertheless, you should keep an eye on things and remark something like, "Boy, you remembered to complete your homework and on time, even though I didn't remind you," or something similar. These few words are a type of praise that may be very reassuring to a child. Remember, if you want to foster a particular behavior in your kid, "catch them being good" by recognizing it.

When you comment on and describe clearly actually a specific behavior that shows their capability, your kids are more likely to adopt that message into their self-view. On a deeper level, they become more aware and accepting of their strengths and abilities. So the child who actually picks up his toys may begin to think of himself as a helper or a cooperative family member who contributes.

By giving your kids distinct positive images of themselves, you are equipping them to deal with some of the challenges they may encounter in the "outside world." Specific, sincere praise is part of conscious parenting. It can be hard work, and it also requires practice, but the pay-off over time is tremendous. Praise can impact how children feel about themselves. So you want to roll out the right kind. Remember that each kid is an individual and will respond to praise in a different manner based on his or her temperament.

Improving Self-esteem in Three Steps

Improving self-esteem is a complex process, requiring acceptance and change. Though it may take time to actually realize these improvements, the point is to never give up. Each person has something special to offer, and just because you cannot see it now doesn't mean it's not there. All you need to do is find what works for you. Here are three steps that can help you become more confident in your strengths and skills.

Step 1 – Remove the Inner Critic

Criticism is a part of life. When approached in a positive manner, it can help a person evolve. However, people with low self-esteem are usually their own worst critics and are generally unreceptive to criticism from others, especially if it's negative. Maybe you don't realize what they are yet, but certain situations in your life need to be handled differently. You need to stop focusing solely on the negative aspects and start seeing the positive ones. Only by doing this can you objectively analyze your progress.

As a result, there are certain behaviors in particular that may need to be corrected:

Many people are afraid of public speaking, and even well-prepared speakers may face butterflies in their stomachs. However, this is a skill that can be learned through practice. When you first address a group of people, you can see right away if the message is well-received or if they are bored. When you feel that everything is going according to plan, don't sabotage your achievement. There may be flaws in your speech, but in most cases, you're the only one who observes them. Use them as strengths to become better and better, and not as a source of criticism.

Being unable to actually complete a task doesn't mean all you have achieved so far is worthless. Being too harsh on yourself can visibly influence your work in a negative way. Remember, it's impossible to know everything, and you can always ask for help with a problem.

Recognizing that you are having trouble doing something doesn't make you a loser; it may actually help you seek help, overcome obstacles, and evolve as a person.

People with low self-esteem have the tendency to be negative about almost everything. They always feel that it's their fault when something goes wrong. Using these assumptions as a crutch will not help you solve your issues. You can't blame yourself for what others are feeling. Sometimes situations don't work out the way you intended. You need to focus on yourself and what you can bring to the table.

Love is a sensible subject. It's never pleasant to be turned down or end a relationship. At first, both seem like catastrophic situations that couldn't possibly lead to anything good. Setbacks in the dating world shouldn't allow you to forget who you are. If something goes wrong, you need to analyze what was good and what was bad about the situation, learn from the experience, and move on. Living in the past or assuming you'll never find someone else who loves you will increase your negativity and lower your self-esteem – and who wants to be around someone like that? Having a calm, mature, and positive attitude will help you learn from the situation and hopefully avoid making the same mistakes twice.

Step 2 – Practice Empathy

Once you begin to get rid of your hyper-critical inner voice, you're ready to see yourself in a more positive light. This means you have strengths and weaknesses like anyone else, and there are still some things in every life that may be hard to handle. Acknowledging this is key. You need to provide positive support for yourself and think encouraging thoughts. It's good to evaluate yourself, but it's also extremely important to take a break from and avoid being overly critical. You don't need to place yourself in constant competition with others. This can be very tiring, and in many cases it's completely useless. Take a break, relax, and consider the possibilities.

There will be moments when you have many things on your mind, and you're unable to finish everything you plan. This is not a reason to feel bad, but rather a good opportunity to analyze the situation in a positive manner. If the urgent matters are solved first, you're already a winner. Such situations are inevitable, but recognizing your limits and accepting them will do wonders for future situations.

It's vital to acknowledge that making mistakes is natural. Everybody does it, and this doesn't mean they are failures. Instead of blaming yourself for something that went wrong, you need to recognize and to try to fix it. Irritation needs to be replaced with compassion.

Increasing your self-esteem means embracing emotions without allowing them to alter your thoughts. It's not wrong to feel sorrow or joy, envy or satisfaction. They're all part of our human nature. Repressing them can make you feel overwhelmed, and this can have a terrible effect on your confidence. Be comfortable embracing your emotions. Life is too short!

Step 3 – Accept Help

The last and possibly the hardest step to learn is to accept help from others. You may feel you don't deserve it, that it's an admission of failure or would mean losing your competitive edge. It's true that not all people have good intentions. If you analyze your situation well, you will find people that you can rely on.

Here are a few ways you can reach out the right people:

The people who care most about you are your family. Don't feel embarrassed about talking to loved ones about your problems because they'll be glad to help. They love you, right? More than anything, they're going to be happy to see you smile again.

Friends are another great resource. You can ask for advice or simply talk about your feelings. Hearing them tell you what a great friend you are and receiving a hug after your talk will make you feel confident again.

Some people may find it too hard to open their hearts to family and friends. The actual best solution is to talk to a therapist or a counselor. It's very difficult to deal with low self-esteem, especially when you can't manage to find the root of your problems. There's no shame in asking a professional for help, and many thousands of trained experts are out there, ready to listen and help you tackle your issues.

Improving self-esteem and building confidence is a complex process. It requires eliminating the critical inner voice, adopting a compassionate attitude towards yourself, and talking about your feelings with others. Though it may seem impossible to achieve in the beginning, loved ones, friends, and even professional counselors can help you learn more about who you are and how much you are valued.

Chapter 21
Practical Steps to Building Self-Esteem in Children

At this point, you are well acquainted with self-esteem. You also know what to look out for when watching for a change in your child's self-esteem. However, knowing the problem is but one part of the puzzle. Knowing how to solve it is the other part, and it is the most important. In this chapter, you will learn practical steps to building healthy self-esteem in your children.

First, what's so good about healthy self-esteem? Well, there are quite a lot of benefits. A healthy self-esteem helps kids cope with their mistakes. With a healthy dose of self-confidence, they often try again and again, even if they have failed once. It helps them build a backbone, which will become handy when they grow up and face bigger challenges. Also, children with healthy self-esteem do better in academics. They take criticism well because they don't believe it is an attack on their person and, hence, they grow.

Helping your children build healthy self-esteem is a worthy investment of time and effort, as your children would grow to be the best versions of themselves and make you so proud. So, how do you go about building self-esteem in children? Here are some practical steps you can start doing today and begin to see results.

Show them love

Children with low self-esteem often feel unloved. So, show them you love them and that you are their number one cheerleader. Always tell them about how much you love them, give gifts, and become interested in their lives.

Praise them genuinely

Praise them when they make little strides. Be genuine and do not be patronizing. If they sense that you are patronizing them, you will get the opposite effect. Tell them how smart they are and how proud you are of them. It is not only when they get good grades or do something wonderful; praise them when they fail and acknowledge their effort while telling them you are proud of them because you know they will try again.

Praising your child can be a double-edged sword if not applied at the right time. Do not deliver praise when your kids do commonplace things like waking up early. It defeats the purpose of delivering the praise. Be sure not to over praise such that you feed the child the wrong sense of pride. For instance, Diego has always played the violin with his father, a retired celebrity violinist. Every time he played, his father heaped praise on him and made him feel like the world had never seen a violinist like him. This made Diego feel too confident in his skills. However, when he grew and applied to join a music school with very high achievers in the music world, he found out that although he was good, he wasn't as good as his father made him out to be. He was in a mess because his father could have given him criticisms and he would have bettered his craft, instead of finding out on a bigger stage.

Avoid harsh criticism

When criticizing your child, make it constructive and avoid the use of harsh words, as this destroys any self-confidence built. Desist from comparing your child to his peers in the name of criticism. This damages his self-esteem more than you would ever know.

Step back

Instead of always trying to help your child or heaping him with praise all the time, step back and allow him to sort out things for himself. When he learns things on his own, it helps him build competence and then more confidence in his abilities. In clearer terms, allow your child to take risks, solve problems, and figure things out on his own.

Allow them makes their choices

Always making choices for them takes away from their own capabilities and erodes their self-confidence. When kids make their own age-appropriate choices, they feel more powerful.

Allow them pursue their own interests

Another surefire technique to develop confidence in children is to encourage them to embark on chores that they are interested in doing themselves. Then make certain that they follow through. The job might be anything from swimming laps to defeating levels in video games; it is all up to the individual. The goal is to remain with what they've started so they may have a sense of success at the conclusion of the process.

Make sure your child's goals are within a level appropriate for his ability

I may be necessary to advise a child to join a league, where he may feel like a star rather than the last one chosen for the AA squad. When MacLeod's son, Alex, was in second grade, she learnt this lesson the hard way. Alex was about to give up on reading after feeling like a failure until MacLeod brought home some Magic Tree House books that were just a little over Alex's reading level. According to her, "He read one every two days and was so happy of himself that he went on to actually read the Goosebumps series with no issue." Following the game, Alex's mother and son discussed how Alex's decision to train had paid off, and she commended him for his tenacity.

Checklist for Building Self-esteem in your Children

It is critical for you to assist your children in discovering their own unique abilities and attributes, as well as recognizing and appreciating their strengths. In short, make them feel special. However, they should be taught that feeling exceptional does not always imply feeling better than others. Make a list of your objectives. Instill in your children the actual importance of working toward a goal and taking pleasure in their achievements. Ensure that they have opportunity for achievement. Try and try again. Encourage your children to experiment with different approaches, to confront obstacles, and to take chances.

Building self-esteem and self-confidence is quite easy. You just have to know what you are doing. Cheers to building kids who have a healthy dose of self-esteem and are poised to do great things now and in the future.

Chapter 22
How We Influence Our Child's Self-Esteem

If we return to the 2001 Joseph Rowntree Foundation's audit of studies on kids' confidence, it calls attention to "The most grounded impacts upon confidence are the singular's folks." That should highlight the significance of what we are going to set out on. Having an arrangement is significant; however, having the right intent to help your kid's confidence is fundamental. My framework will assist your kids with understanding the positive self-esteem they have the right to have. The guardians should be a vital piece of the whole process.

How this Program is Different

My program depends on building confidence through solid living. It relates to the association of the psyche and body, joining together for an uplifting perspective off our youngsters. We aren't having a profound otherworldly and philosophical discussion here; we are attempting to assist them with ameliorating a significant part of the antagonism related with a lower self-esteem. I seek to give parents a deep rooted way to deal with keeping the confidence in your youngster's life. It is a program they use even into adulthood. This program will show methods for dealing with stress and how youngsters view themselves and the world around them.

The Role of Parents

Parents it can roll out enormous improvements in your own lives along with their children's. All things that are considered, if your confidence is low, how might you help your child? Parents need to take an interest in this arrangement – very much like your youngsters should. Being a positive example is critical. Your youngster won't become tied into the program if you won't.

You can receive the rewards of positive confidence by acquiring amazing propensities in your life. One will be the rising confidence of your child and two, you will emerge as a superior individual yourself.

The Role of the Mind and Body

The brain and body have a basic association – one assuredly influences the other. The solidarity of the psyche and body are significant in aiding youngsters gain and keep their confidence. This diminishes pressure and permits the legitimate capacity of the kid's body.

Using the body (through Yoga, Tai chi, etc.) to create a relaxed state reduces stress and helps the child (and you) develop a positive state of mind. Once you reach this positive state of mind, it helps your child deal with many of the negative situations that they encounter throughout their lives.

You may be thinking, "Yoga, Meditation or Tai chi for my kids?" I'm not looking at doing a full Bikram Yoga meeting, yet essentially extending, breathing, and delivering oneself of pessimistic considerations isn't that hard for a youngster to comprehend and execute – particularly with the assistance of the parent. You are establishing the framework for a positive body and soul. The capacity to keep a positive brain and body association will endure forever in your youngsters and give them a springboard for more prominent things to come.

How My Plan Helps your Child

Providing your kids with the fundamental components of positive psyche and body association will help their confidence. Here is a framework for every one of the positive propensities I need you and your children to embrace, and what it can mean for the self-esteem.

Habit 1 – Nourish your body

This is critical, as an ever increasing number of studies show an expansion of confidence in well-fed children. While heftiness itself doesn't really prompt low confidence, it can bring down the youngster's mental self-view and subsequently propel them to a lower self-esteem. Eating the right food assists with keeping a proper weight, while it additionally promotes general wellbeing and helps keep the resistance framework of the body rolling to battle disease. Keeping the body brimming with sustenance is a significant component in my program. It is the first step.

Habit 2 – Exercise

Stress is not something to be thankful for, particularly if you are a child. Restricting a kid's pressure with normal exercise should shrewdly consolidate the youngster's brain and body. Furthermore, practice keeps the body running and permits the kid to work on their confidence through movement. The body delivers specific endorphins to conquer and avoid sentiments related to nervousness and depression.

Habit 3 – Get enough rest

Many individuals debate the significance of legitimate rest for themselves and their youngsters too. Truth be told, legitimate rest helps in managing life's circumstances, reducing a drop in confidence. Sleep renews the body and empowers it – two critical components in keeping a brain and body balance.

Habit 4 – Integrate the body and mind

One of the fundamental parts of the body and psyche association is mindfulness and solace. Understanding your body and being on top of it is a fundamental stage in my program – and in building self-esteem. Once somebody understands that they reserve the option to encounter psyche and body congruity, they are equipped to take care of stressful circumstances and the associated tension with a superior attitude (e.g. the development of the body and various attributes, etc.)

Habit 5 – Clearing your issues

Our current world is brimming with negative circumstances; things from a while ago and as well as recent developments. As grown-ups, we make intense memories and have to deal, so envision how our youngsters feel about this.

Some individuals ceaselessly experience adverse circumstances, and many accept this is a consequence of not relinquishing negativing and pondering more positive results. You must be leery of arrival of these negative sentiments and permit the positive ones to come in. by binding the body and the mind as a unit. Meditation is one method of getting issues out of the psyche, making for harmony in the body. This lets pressure off and takes into account the role of self-esteem.

Habit 6 – Change Your Thoughts

We are largely liable for how we feel – no other person can make a case for that. But our youngsters frequently take on the sentiments and mentalities of the people around them. As parents, we can show them that they have command over how they feel and the circumstances they are in. If we think negatively, then negativity is going to overtake our bodies and minds.

Take the 11-year-old kid once more. He may accept that he isn't acknowledged by others since he is on the huge side. When he accepts and acknowledges it and recognizes that he brings a lot to the table for other children, his confidence rises.

Habit 7 – Cultivate a loving, positive relationship

Once again the job of the parent comes to the fore. We can affect our youngsters simply by the manner we identify with them in our everyday living. It includes everything from how we discipline them to extending admiration and appreciation while giving applause. It is all pivotal in bringing up a kid who is glad and sound– and in particular with a higher self-esteem!

Taking Responsibility

Do you recall the first time you held your baby in your arms? You swore to yourself that you would let no harm come to them. Ever since, you have loved them unconditionally, watched them grow, cried with them when they were hurt, played nonsensical games for hours, worried about their health, nutrition, and well-being, helped them crawl, stand, and walk on their two feet, and offered them comfort and your warm embrace whenever they came crying to you. As parents, we all want to nurture our kids, keep them safe from harm, and teach them the best values so when they grow up, they are ready for the world.

But while doing so, we have - and we are talking about every parent here - sometimes we have shielded them from making mistakes. We have come to the rescue even before they did something wrong or harmful. Although you aren't to blame here, did you know that whenever you did that, you deprived them of a great learning opportunity to grow and build resilience (Oosthuizen, 2020)? To raise them as healthy, capable, emotionally-intellectual, and confident individuals, we have to let them make mistakes. But, of course, own up to them too!

When do children make mistakes? When they do something the way it shouldn't be done. Usually, errors result in failure, which leads to stress and the buildup of negative emotions. But despite that, children must be given every opportunity to struggle so even if they fail, they develop emotional and coping skills. Many psychologists associate coping skills with muscles. We can never know how strong we are unless we use them.

Historically, many educators believe that to perfect one's skill development, the best way is to eliminate mistakes. It made sense for some time, and many educators followed suit; but things started to change when researchers and child specialists observed how crucial a role mistakes play in fostering resilience. Even today, we don't deliberately set up our kids for failure. We have this premeditated notion to make things easier for them so they do without mistakes.

Unconsciously, we all discourage mistakes as we feel it is synonymous with failure. So, we drill the right answers into them by repeating the question over and over again until they memorize it and then pray that they do well in a standardized test. Because God forbid, who can afford poor grades even though the child has zero knowledge about the concepts and foundation of things?

Recent studies suggest that learning improves when kids make mistakes as their curiosity to know what is right is heightened. Every form of learning is enriched via error. Ask yourself if they don't choose the wrong friends first, how will they know how to choose the right ones? If they won't wear the left shoe on their right foot and fall, how will they know to put the right shoe on the right foot the next time? Making mistakes challenges kids to do better. Rarely do mistakes result in them giving up. Mistakes motivate them to think differently and come up with a new possible solution or explanation for things. It makes their minds go in turbo-charge mode to attempt things differently. Isn't that what learning should look like? It should be fun, challenging, and a driving force to discover new possibilities and approaches.

According to Carol Dweck, the author of the bestseller, Mindset: The New Psychology of Success, and a professor at Stanford University, children must always be challenged one way or another to enhance learning. Even when they repeatedly make mistakes, parents shouldn't try to make things easier rather let them come up with new strategies and the means to handle them. Her research suggests that when parents repetitively praise children for their intelligence rather than their problem-solving skills, they are less likely to persist in the face of a challenge? This conclusion was derived after her team of experts followed up on 100+ 5th graders in the best schools of NYC. She writes about the experiment in detail to encourage parents to praise kids over their efforts – even if they fail – and not their intelligence, which happens to be a genetic trait. To briefly sum up her experiment, she divided the participating 5th graders into two groups. One group was appreciated for their intelligence while the other for their effort.

As it turns out, when faced with a challenging test designed for 8th graders, children praised for their efforts performed harder despite making numerous mistakes. They seemed more determined to take on the task and tried their best to perform better. On the other hand, children who were praised for their intelligence soon felt like failures as the more mistakes they made, the more discouraged they got.

This proved that parents who praise results more than efforts don't raise resilient kids. Instead, they raise kids who are too scared to disappoint such that they don't even give their best shot at things. Therefore, if you are doing the same, you can't expect your offspring to grow up to become resilient as they lack the skills to accept failure and come out of it. Moreover, Dweck also believes parents shouldn't be too quick to praise or put down their children as they lose important opportunities for learning.

Did I Do Something Wrong?

A mistake can be anatomized as a decision or action we soon come to regret. Mistakes come paired with some form of loss, pain, and struggle. No not even adults are in favor of the consequences. But that doesn't mean we never regret our actions. We all do! Sometimes, graver ones are made by our kids. But the irony is that mistakes are one of the things we try hard not to stumble upon and yet, sometimes, they are also the most important things we need to experience.

As we don't like to be reminded of our mistakes from time to time, so don't our kids. Parents who have the habit of bringing up their children's mistakes in front of others to joke or ridicule them are setting them up for poor self-worth and low self-esteem. Kids who are often mocked by one or both their parents exhibit unstable mental health as they feel they are not good enough. As parents, we shouldn't bring up past mistakes to degrade our kids. As already established, making mistakes can be good, but we have to format our responses accordingly.

Watching our kids make a blunder or two is never easy. Knowing what they are actually doing is wrong, it is hard to resist the temptation to make things better for them. Of course, your instinct is to save them from trauma, pain, or hurt, but perhaps it is best to let them navigate their own way. When they spring back from mistakes with techniques they came up with, it boosts their sense of confidence. So, instead of focusing solely on what they did wrong, try to focus on helping them cope with the emotions that follow. How will they cope with anger, frustration, or guilt after they have made a mistake? Well, that is where you step in. But before we actually do that, make sure you do the following:

Say Thank You

If they come to you to admit they have made a boo-boo, thank them for it. Of course, it will boil your blood when they tell you what they have done, but this is the moment when you have to overlook the mistake and praise them for their honesty. This gives children an open window for communication as they feel they can come up to you with whatever troubles them and be expressive about it. This also teaches them that you will offer help rather than a sound scolding, which instills the idea that they always have someone they can count on.

Encourage Risk-Taking

Your kid should try something new every day to broaden their knowledge. They shouldn't worry about making mistakes or be afraid of failure. Show them it is okay to step out of their comfort zones and give new things a try.

Be Vocal About Their Efforts

If you have only been praising them over an A+ grade or winning a spelling, you are amplifying their fear of trying new things. They start to believe that if they try something new, they will surely fail. This makes them dependent and less resilient. So, applaud their efforts even if they fail to achieve the desired results. This will make them persistent and more willing to take on new challenges.

Tell Them a Secret

To instill the habit of owning up to mistakes, share the mistakes you made when you were their age and how you coped. Tell them in detail how you handled them, owned up them, and made the required compensations to prevent repeating them. When kids make mistakes, they feel like failures. They think they are incapable of handling things. But having someone tell them they aren't the only ones to make mistakes fills them with a sense of comfort and gives them a boost to do better.

Teach Them Accountability

One of the greatest things one can do when they have faulted is to accept responsibility for their actions and be accountable. In case our mistakes have hurt someone, it is our job to apologize. Your kids should be taught the same from an early age so they learn an important life lesson – fix something that has been broken at the right time. They must acknowledge that their actions resulted in someone getting hurt and, therefore, it is now their job to make amends. This allows them to move past the grief, shame, and guilt they feel. It also shows them that everything can be made better if one tries hard enough.

Teach Them to Trace Back

Kids need to know what mistakes they made. If you want them to claim responsibility for their blunders, ask them what they did and what happened afterward. Remind them to trace it back and know what action resulted in the mistake, so the next time they avoid repeating it.

Tell Them What's Done Is Done

There is no point in holding on to faults. Kids shouldn't think that just because they have made a mistake, it is the end of the world. Instead, tell them it is just the beginning of learning. For example, if they lost a race on sports day, instead of putting them down, encourage them to try harder the next time, get a coach, or try a different technique. But be mindful as you don't want to hand them the solutions on a plate; you need to encourage them to brainstorm ideas themselves.

Be Their Accountability Partner

If you want them to avoid repeating the same mistakes over and over, someone has to keep them in check and navigate their way. Be their accountability partner so you remain aware that they haven't fully given up something because they made a blunder and remind them to work harder as you are counting on them. Create chore lists and place them in visible places where they see them. Be sure to mention the mistake they made in a subtle but clear manner. For example, if the last time they forgot to separate their laundry into white and blacks, a little reminder suggesting to sort properly can go a long way.

Discipline

Discipline is often a negative word because, especially for children, it involves punishment. To discipline a child is to teach him a code to help him become a responsible adult. Discipline may include praise, criticism and feedback as well as punishment. Praise can be a powerful tool for disciplining children. Praise your children when they do something right. They will be more inclined to do it again.

You will have to decide what punishment you want. I am not here to discuss the spank/no spank issue. Some of these tips touch on possible options and ways to deal with punishment. Critiquing is telling your daughter what went wrong and feedback is telling how to make it right. Both accomplish the same task, but the recipient will feel better and more likely to follow through with feedback than critics.

Knowing the difference and using feedback more often help you have more constructive and respectful conversations.

Compliment Often

Always compliment your child. No matter if Jenny was late for school or didn't hang up her clothes, compliment her and say thank you. Positive reinforcement is the best way to sustain good behavior. Children thrive on compliments. We all love them. Focus your compliments on the areas they control. It's better to praise her for the way she has brushed her hair and dressed herself than to just say that she looks beautiful. It's better to praise her study skills than tell her that she got an A on her test.

Be careful not to praise and compliment Jenny so often and so frequently that it loses its meaning. It's not a good idea to constantly tell Jenny she is "wonderful" and "super". After a while, it loses its magic. She will take you more seriously if you praise specific actions and attributes. An honest compliment is better than any criticism.

Be Relaxed, But Always be in charge

There is a distinction between being gentle and being strict. It's not a good idea to be strict with your child, but you don't want her to be too loose. Be casual, approachable, and friendly in your relationship with her. However, if there are rules that must be followed, you should be the one in charge.

Children need to know that you care. When I was fifteen years old, a friend told me her curfew. Her tone of voice, expression and attitude made it clear that she wasn't happy about it. Although she might have argued about a curfew, it was clear that her parents were concerned for her.

You can be so laid back that your child believes you don't care about what they do. They'll take advantage. It's important to let them know that the standards you have set are there because you care about their choices. If you can put it all together as love, they will be more open to your decisions. Rules that are based on love and not power are easier to accept.

Praise Character, as well as Actions

While it is easy to praise the actions of our children, which are often about the good things they do, it can be more difficult to highlight positive character traits. These will help us determine what kind of person he will become. He'll come to believe that he must always be an achiever to get your praise and respect.

Jody may have broken your vase and then admitted it to you right away. You should compliment him for being honest. He will give you a hug if you are feeling sick or tired. When he shares his toy, tell him how thoughtful and kind he is. You will teach him to be compassionate and caring adult without having to preach or explain. A mouthful of praise is worth more than a mouthful lecture.

Offer Suggestions in a Positive Way

There are many "don'ts" in life, and children seem to be more aware of them than anyone else. "Don't get your hands dirty", "Don't let go the kite," and "Don't run in the street." Try to rephrase "don't" in a positive manner if you find yourself repeating the phrase too often. Research has shown that the brain does not process the word "don't". When you say, "Don't get dirty," the brain hears "Get dirty." Positively stating your request will increase the likelihood of positive results. You could use the following examples to say, "Try not to get dirty," "Hold your kite tight," and "Please stay inside the yard." However, the end result is the same: a clean child clinging onto a kite in the yard. The child doesn't feel like he can do anything. You can do the same with either a "do" or a "don't. Always go for the "do".

If you must Criticize, Make it Constructive

You've already put your child on defensive and won the battle. He will not hear what you have to say, even the things you want him change. Instead, suggest a better way of doing something and, if possible, explain how it can benefit him. For example, "Connor," in a friendly tone of voice, "If you do a quick clean-up in your bedroom before you go to sleep each night, you'll be able to have more time for play and less cleaning."

Be careful when you use the word "should". Instead of telling a child what to do, discuss it as if the task is already done. Instead of actually saying "You must clean your room before we go," try saying, "After you have cleaned your room, we'll go." This implies that he will clean his room. Avoid words such as always, never, only, or only (if you would .only..., you never...). These words suggest that the idea is so simple that they should have thought it up. It might sound as if you were saying, "Any dummy knows ...." More cooperation = more pleasant words and neutral voices.

Criticize the Act – Not the Child

"Why are your toilets always so messy?" "Why must you always leave your bathroom so messy?" These statements will make your child feel bad about herself and believe she cannot do better. You're also asking a question, even a rhetorical one, for which there is no right or wrong answer. This puts your child in a losing position. Your criticism should be directed at the bathroom, not the child. "Would it be possible to make the bathroom cleaner after you have finished your shower?" is not a criticism of her personally. Criticizing the child might make her feel that you don't love her. Criticizing the child's behavior will not make her feel you don't love her, especially if your request is followed by, "I love YOU!"

"I don't like what you do but I love who and what you are."

Use I, not You statements

Instead of focusing on her successes, focus on how you feel. Instead of saying, "You are so messy," you could say "I don't like going to the bathroom with wet towels all over the floor" or "You have toothpaste everywhere on the counter." It would be actually nice if it was neater for me." Next, make sure she knows exactly what "neater" means to you. This could be towels hung up or dirty clothes in a hamper.

A statement that begins with "you" can put the other person on defense before they hear the rest. It is worse to say, "You always ..." because it makes the child feel guilty about their actions. Guilt should not be used as a parenting tool. You should not "guilt" your child into doing something. If you use the "I" or state your objection, it is not about what they are doing wrong. It's about how you react to it or what you want to see change. It is small, but it can make a huge difference in how the request will be heard and received.

Correction does much, but encouragement does more. ~ Johann Wolfgang von Goethe

Define Limits and Expectations

Kellen's mother, Kellen, told Kellen to place his dirty socks in the hamper. They were still on her bed when she returned later. After telling him again, she checked back and saw that they were still in the dresser. He was irritated and she told him to get them into the hamper. He looked at her in tears, and asked "Mommy! What's a hamper?"

Children acquire vocabulary quickly and often forget that they might not be able to understand certain words. They may interpret the meaning of the word differently. For example, the word "clean" may have one meaning to you but a totally different meaning to a three-year-old or even a thirteen year-old. Instead of saying, "Clean your bedroom," tell him to put his toys away and wash the clothes in the hamper. You'll find he will be more open to hearing what you have in mind.

You'll get better results if you can explain the scope, meaning, and limitations of any instruction. You can ask the child to repeat what you said, or you may ask him questions to see if he understands. You can explain to your child what you mean if you aren't sure. If they don't know the terms, they won't be able to follow the rules.

Discipline Calmly, Not in Anger

Anger towards children, especially young ones, can make them feel they are a bad person or that their parents don't care about them. Calm punishment with explanations about why she is being punished sends the message that her behavior is unacceptable. Make sure that she understands why she is being punished and what you expect in the future.

Be gentle with your child when you are disciplining her. Adults can be intimidating enough by being taller than their children. However, if they're angry and tall, it only increases the child's fear. Talk calmly but firmly and get on her level. To reassure her about your love and commitment, end the time-out or discussion with a hug.

Great anger can be more destructive than the sword. ~ Tamil proverb

Replace Scolding with Requests

As adults, we sometimes use our power to nag, scold, and belittle our children because we are the grownups. We wouldn't treat a guest in the same manner. Instead of shouting, "Don't leave the dirty glasses on the table!" instead say, "Please place them in the dishwasher." This achieves the same result without making the child they've made a mistake. If they are caught putting the glass into the dishwasher, praise them or say "Thanks, I appreciate that!"

A smile and a "Thank You" will help you make the desired action a habit. It sets a good example for family members to use "Please" or "Thank you" even when they are not present! Children are people, too. They appreciate being treated with kindnesses and respect.

Avoid Negative Labels

Negative labels are one of the most harmful and damaging things that we can do in reaction to our child's actions or behavior. It does not help to tell a child that she is stupid, lazy, irresponsible or clumsy. It is more likely to encourage it. Avoid using negative words for the child. Labels can be used to highlight positive attributes and behaviors. Then, find the words to describe them. Keep your eyes on what they can control.

Although telling your son that he is cute or handsome will not hurt him and may boost his self-esteem, it won't make him feel he has contributed to it. But if you tell him he's clever for having figured out how to fix his bike, you're complimenting his skill, problem-solving abilities, and persistence that he can control and strengthen. Negative labels are never justified.

Determine your Discipline Style

It is difficult enough for a child to know what is right and wrong without being caught up in her parents' interpretations. There will be clashes if Dad believes in spanking and Mom is from the "time-out" school of discipline. If Mom insists that the beds must be made every morning no matter what, but Dad tells her to not worry, then what's a child to do? She's likely not going to make her bed. Now Mom is back on her case.

These kinds of fights should not be repeated. It's time for parents to take a step back and make decisions. Each parent must be willing to let go of some of their disciplinary beliefs. If Mom is willing to stop insisting on making the bed, Dad might be able to stop spanking. The child will fight you each against the other no matter what your decisions may be. If parents are not in agreement, the child will take over.

Be Consistent with Discipline

Consistency is another important factor. Bobby will not be able to understand what you are doing if you don't look at him one time and then give ground the next. Make a rule and enforce it. You must enforce it every time...almost without exceptions because sometimes, unavoidable events do occur - I say almost. He doesn't deserve to get punished if he is late due to running out of gas. If it is true, he shouldn't be punished. Yet he's old enough to drive, it's possible to read the gas gauge and take preventative measures to avoid running out. Be fair, firm, and consistent.

Avoid Over-Reacting to Minor Infractions

It is not possible to raise a perfect child. Accept the fact that she may make mistakes, forget to feed the cat, or break some dishes. These aren't major flaws in her personality! You can scream at her or punish her for these kinds of misdeeds. But later, when she is older, you will need to make a case for something much bigger (sneaking out at 14, taking the car and knocking over a lamp post). It won't seem as wrong to her as leaving a wet towel on floor. It is okay to ask her to be more careful when washing dishes. Tell her to grab the towel and remind her that she needs to feed the cat. You'll lose credibility later if you react too quickly.

Pay attention to what happens when you react to the unexpected. Although this can be difficult, it is essential to maintain clear and open communication. Take a deep breath and some time to reflect on the issue. You can always handle it: there are solutions for every problem. However, you won't be able to solve them or even discuss them if your thinking isn't clear. You'll be better prepared to confront the problem if you have a few moments alone. You'll be more able to talk about it calmly and rationally when you return. Your child will also feel better.

You'll show your children early that you are able to take difficult news and questions without panicking. This will help them trust you when they face the bigger issues. You'll be able to trust them and they won't become depressed, angry, or hysterical.

When love and faith are involved, nothing is impossible.

Make the Punishment Fit the Offense

It's quite extreme to ground Rachel if she continues to watch TV after you ask her to complete a chore. However, if Rachel took your expensive camera and broke it, she isn't strong enough to learn right from wrong. If possible, make a connection between the punishment and the infraction. You could either take Rachel's TV privileges away for the remainder of the day or make her dust the room every other day. The camera should be taken apart and Rachel made to pay for the repair or replacement. This could prove costly.

Consider how serious the offense is. There are consequences for your actions. Bad actions can have severe consequences.

Choose your Battles

Do not stress about whether Sage eats all his vegetables or Sadie wears red socks and blue socks. Stick to what is most important. Make sure you enforce any rule that you have. But don't make it so complicated that it is impossible to follow all of them. You can focus on the small things like what they should eat or wear (as long they are actually getting the nutrition they require) and how much order they should have in their lives.

As long as the hospital doesn't actually have to intervene, there is room.

Instead of focusing on chores, focus on the battles for character. It is better to insist that they are honest and responsible, rather than that their bed has been made or that their clothes match. These insignificant matters will make it easier to enforce the more important ones, such as hygiene, homework, and honesty.

Sometimes the end result doesn't justify fighting.

Chapter 23
How to Build Resilience in Children

Parents frequently inquire about resilience, particularly when their children are experiencing difficulties in school, their self-esteem, or keeping friendships. This chapter will look at the characteristics that must be present for children to develop resilience and practical solutions for parents and caregivers to use.

Resilience is defined as a person's ability to cope with hardship and bounce back from traumatic experiences. When a youngster successfully overcomes a problem, they feel a sense of accomplishment. This achievement assists children in developing confidence in their abilities and preparing them to confront difficulties in the future. Homework, establishing friends, moving to a new house, changes in schools, bullying, parent separation, or even death are just a few examples of obstacles that may arise. Children who can bounce back from these situations will grow. Additionally, it enables them to endure and "give it another shot" when things don't go their way.

Developing resilience can be learned by anyone at any age, and it is not dependent on a child's abilities or personality. According to research, resilience can lower the likelihood of developing childhood sadness and anxiety, reduce the chance of developing adult mental health difficulties, and can be a predictor of success in school or the workplace Having a resilient child means they can cope better with the events that occur throughout their life, are better able regulate their behavior and manage after experiencing traumatic situations.

To help your child develop resilience, you can use a variety of approaches. The tactics listed below are evidence-based, although some may be more appropriate for your circumstance depending upon your child's interests and strengths, and your parenting style. If your child currently has excellent communication abilities, concentrate on a method that will help them improve in an area they haven't yet mastered.

Why Resilience Good for Children?

Resilient children can bounce back from setbacks and go back to living their lives. When kids overcome setbacks and issues, it boosts their confidence and makes them feel more capable the next time they face a challenge. Resilient children are frequently adept at fixing issues and picking up new abilities. This is due to their willingness to try again if things don't go as planned the first time.

When things don't go as planned and the child experiences anxiety, sadness, disappointment, fear, or frustration, resilience helps them learn that these unpleasant feelings don't endure forever. They may go through these feelings and know that everything will be ok in the end. Resilient children are less likely to ignore difficulties or react in negative ways, such as becoming defensive or violent or injuring themselves purposely. Resilient youngsters are more likely to have good physical and mental health than children who are not. Children develop resilience as a result of their experiences. Your child's confidence in their capacity to tackle the next task grows with each difficulty solved.

You can Increase your Child's Resiliency through the following Strategies:

Encourage your child, but refrain from resolving every minor issue or disappointment. If your child isn't invited to a birthday party or doesn't get what they want for their birthday, instead of attempting to remedy the situation, you may speak about how they feel.

Predicting and avoiding troubles for your child should be avoided. This might include not repairing a broken item or allowing your child to give in incorrect schoolwork. Overcoming small obstacles strengthens your child's resilience in the face of larger setbacks.

Assist your youngster in recognizing and managing powerful emotions. For example, your youngster may be concerned about a sick family member. "I see you're concerned about Grandpa," you could say. "It's fine to be concerned. But keep in mind that we're doing everything we can to assist him in getting healthy."

You should encourage your child to try again if something doesn't work out the first time. Praise your youngster for trying, regardless of the outcome. You may say something like, "I'm proud of you for finishing the marathon" or "Well done for trying again."

Develop your child's sense of self-compassion. Self-compassion encourages your kid to be nice to themselves in the face of sadness, failure, or mistakes. This enhances their ability to move on from unfavorable circumstances.

Make it a practice to notice and appreciate positive developments. You may, for example, share one positive item from your day at family dinners.

Assist your child in developing the age-appropriate problem-solving abilities. Consider how your child could react if a youngster at school says or does anything nasty to him or her in the future.

Look for a positive role model who has faced comparable difficulties as your child. Your youngster, for example, could find comfort in an older buddy whose parents have divorced or who has just lost a family member.

Creating a Strong Bond with your Child

A child's resilience is based on their ability to form strong, healthy relationships with adults. As a result, focusing on your relationship with your child will aid in the development of resilience. Active listening skills, being aware of your child's needs and reacting consistently, and spending time with your child while enjoying their favorite activities all help to strengthen attachment.

Taking on Responsibilities

Household chores can be an excellent method to foster self-esteem, independence, pride in one's work, self-assurance in one's abilities, and a sense of belonging and value to one's family. Chore rewards don't necessarily have to be money or candy. Instead, consider rewarding yourself with things like picking the movie for family movie night or Sunday dinner. These forms of rewards encourage a youngster to internalize his or her accomplishments rather than relying on external rewards such as money to recognize them.

Develop Emotional Self-Control

Most children can recognize the emotions of happiness, sadness, frustration, and anger, but they may struggle to understand why they are frustrated, what happens to their bodies when they are annoyed, and what they can do to heal themselves. "I see you're furious because you're shouting and your fists are clinched," rather than "Don't be rude to him" or "Stop yelling at him," try to help them identify and regulate their emotions by saying something like, "I see you're angry because you're shouting and your fists are clenched." Because Tom took the train, you're enraged. "I understand that you're unpleasantly stressed today because you're becoming frustrated," or "I know your homework is stressful today because you're getting frustrated" is a better way to encourage Tom to stop or obtain help. Do you want to take a break or do you need some assistance?"

The child learns about their emotions, emotion control, and problem-solving skills by connecting the cause and feeling and identifying an alternate action. As your child's understanding grows, you may find that they learn to recognize their emotions more quickly and build their own self-regulation strategy.

Participation of the Community

Community participation has been identified as a protective element in the development of resilience. When a child fails academically or is bullied yet enjoys sports, its common advice to enroll them in sports lessons. This enhances the chances of the children succeeding and putting their resilience abilities to use. Encourage your child to inform their instructors and peers about their accomplishments in sports, music and dance concerts, volunteering, or fundraising activities as another method. This enables the child to carry over the positive feedback from the good circumstance to bad conditions.

Mindfulness

According to research, mindfulness not only increases children's resilience but also reduces parent stress. Mindfulness induces structural and functional changes in the brain that help the body respond to stress in a healthful way. As a result, it increases activity in the prefrontal cortex, which is calming and logical, while decreasing activity in the amygdale, which is instinctual and anxious. The prefrontal cortex and amygdale are also strengthened as a result.

Encourage your Youngster to Seek Assistance

Children frequently recognize that they require assistance but lack the skills to ask for it effectively. For example, a child who informs a teacher that another student is behaving badly may be punished for "tattle-telling." The teacher is more likely to offer problem-solving assistance if the child can explain the same issue, such as "Ben is taunting me and I need help because I don't know what to do next." The teacher's response will also assist the youngster in determining what to do in future conflict situations.

Role play to see how your child begs for help and ask questions like, "What do you think the other person would say if you said this?" or "what happened the last time you attempted this?" Role playing situations such as friendship troubles has been demonstrated to promote confidence, planning, and reduce impulsivity.

Setting Objectives

Encourage your children to make a plan if the difficulty is too great. Begin by creating goals for highly driven tasks such as baking a chocolate cake or figuring out how to beat a difficult level on a computer game, and then apply what they've learned to less compelling chores such as studying for a speech or confronting a bully. Don't discourage them from setting lofty objectives; instead, assist them in determining whether their plans are feasible and provide positive feedback for their achievements. If a plan doesn't work out, go through it again and see what you can do better next time. SMART planning are the most effective (Specific, Measurable, Active, Reachable, Timed).

Creating Models for our Strategies

Allow your children to see your daily problems and how you deal with them. You may, for example, show them how you rehearse what you'll say to someone in the car or before a mirror. Let them see your deep breathing, writing a to-do list or action plan, or practicing self-care to recover from a difficult day. Modeling normalizes the fact that everyone faces obstacles, and your children will be more likely to apply similar techniques as a result. Identify characters that exhibit resilience in your child's favorite books, TV shows, or movies and ask, "How would this character actually act in the same situation?"

Using Technology to Build Resilience

As technology advances and our children become more engaged in online learning, it is critical to foster strong resilience skills for dealing with online bullying as well as self-discipline in terms of how much time they spend online. Being genuinely curious about your child's online habits is a good place to start for parents. For instance, if anything noteworthy happened on social media, if there were any images from the latest party, or if finding information for their scientific assignment was difficult.

These discussions pave the way for future debates on internet security and resilience. When setting technology limits, it's helpful to explain why, for example, "We don't have screen time after 8 p.m. because the backlit screen disrupts our normal sleep cycle." This environment will help a child accept the limitations, gain awareness, and develop their own self-discipline when it comes to screen usage.

Encouragement

Sometimes, the words "praise" or "encouragement" are used interchangeably. However, encouragement and praise are interchangeable. While praise is usually expressed in kind words for something done, encouragement suggests someone do something or be something. To boost morale, encouragement can be used even after a defeat. Although criticism, feedback, feedback and other forms are all important in changing the behavior of a child, encouragement is a much better way to achieve the desired goal.

William Arthur Ward once said, "Flatter you and I may believe you." Criticize me and you may not like me. Ignore me and I might not forgive you. Encourage me, and ...." I won't forget you. It's true, we remember those who have supported us in our journey through life. Encouragement is the best gift you can give to your child, next only to love.

Encourage New Experiences

Although insisting that Freddie eat every bit of his liver won't win you any points, encouraging Freddie at least to taste the strawberry yogurt might have a surprise result. Children and adults can easily get stuck in the same routine. Your children should have a wide range of experiences, but you shouldn't force them to do something.

You could listen to CDs while driving, including country, Cajun, and classical music. Instead of them dismissing it, encourage them to listen. Because we played a variety music on our trips to school, my children learned to love Simon & Garfunkel and Ravel's Bolero equally. Try a museum next time you go to the park every Saturday. It doesn't matter if they love it or not, but they should try other activities to at least know if they enjoy it. Even if they don't, it might help them plant the seeds for the future. Be supportive if they are open to trying new things.

Experimenting with new experiences and adventures builds confidence.

Help Develop Skills and Talents

While trying to discover their passions and talents, children will experience many "wannabe" moments. Encourage them to explore their interests and discover their talents. Encourage them to keep their promises and take on the responsibilities. You must recognize that children will lose interest in many activities as they mature. It is possible for you to not be able fund all their needs: drums, pianos, costumes, and sports equipment can all be quite expensive! Encourage them to explore their interests and make them pay some of the costs. This will help them determine their heart's desire and how willing they are to sacrifice for their dream. They will be more likely to appreciate their investment if they are willing to put in more.

You should make sure they pursue their dreams, not yours.

Encourage them to Read

Reading can help you gain knowledge and spark new interest in the world. Find out if your child doesn't enjoy reading. You might find that your child doesn't like reading because he is having to struggle. It's important that you find out early if dyslexia, poor sight, or learning disabilities are a problem.

If you have the desire but not the problem, then get together and read. Start by showing him articles that relate to his hobby or helping him to find books that interest you. Show him all the books on the subject, including fiction, biography, statistics, and history if he is a big basketball fan. He might be interested in books you read when he was his age. You could also suggest books you loved as a child and explain why you enjoyed them.

Show him where the books are located in bookstores and libraries. Help him choose the right ones for him. You can also discuss the books with him if you have read them. You'll be able to share some interesting facts about his favorite players, which will make you seem cool. This will help you build trust.

Reading actually opens up the world to a child who is able to read.

Teach Goal-Setting

Even children as young as five can set goals and achieve them. If you encourage them and then give them the satisfaction of reaching their goal, you can set them up for a lifetime of goal-setting. Encourage your children to set goals they know they can achieve, but don't give any help. A six-year old who has a $1.00 weekly allowance could set a goal for saving money by her birthday.

If you are from the "Gold Star" school of rewards, ask your child to set a goal for their child to earn 10 gold stars each week for chores completed or good behavior. For older children, a goal could be to read a certain amount of books per month and get at least two "A's each semester. Or whatever is most important to them. To make it meaningful, the child must set the goal and achieve it by himself. While you can give suggestions and steps, your child should decide how to achieve it. Your role is to praise and encourage.

Confidence will grow in a child who is exposed to many successes.

Encourage when They're Down

We need encouragement when we are at our lowest, feeling like a failure, like no one loves us or that we can't do it right. Children feel this more than adults because they lack the experience to see that "this too shall pass."

Dave doesn't like to hear that he is "over it" or "things will get better tomorrow" when he's feeling down. A simple reminder that he isn't the horrible, unlovable person he thinks he is at the moment will help him to get up again. Encourage him to see all the positive things in his life, but do not deny the problem or event that brought him down. He should be able to see the importance of whatever issue he is dealing with.

It won't make Dave feel better to tell him it's "nothing". This could give him the impression you don't care or understand.

Encourage your child to look at all possible sides of the situation that makes him feel blue.

A encouraging word during failure is more valuable than an hour of praise after success. - Author Unknown

Know the Difference between Encouraging and Coercing

Sometimes we think we are encouraging, but in reality we are nagging. There is a fine line between them. If you aren't sure what role you play, ask yourself, "Is this his goal that I'm encouraging or something that I want him to achieve?"

A friend taught his son Johnny tennis. His dad constantly criticized his technique. Johnny was frustrated and almost gave up. Johnny wanted to have fun and not be a professional player like his father. Remember that encouragement is a form of encouragement, especially if you are helping him with an activity he enjoys and he appreciates your feedback. If he wants to have fun, it's coercion.

Learn the difference and remember to bite your tongue if necessary.

Chapter 24
Always Encourage them to Do their Very Best in All Situations

Do not attempt to compel their cooperation. Children are eager to please their parents or caregivers. You should keep in mind that while they may perform better than you anticipate, they may not perform as well as you would actually like. Communicate your concern to your children and your appreciation for their efforts.

When it comes to kids and self-esteem, the most important thing to remember is that they must believe in themselves. He or she needs to be proud of who they are and feel good about themselves. Whatever anyone else thinks, I couldn't care less. My interest isn't even piqued by academic performance. The fact that they may never practice law or serve as President of the United States makes no difference to me at this point. What do they need if they're the best at what they do and their best effort is always met with approval, right?

No worries, everything will work out perfectly for them! The fact that they may never achieve satisfactory academic results does not bother me. The only thing that will actually make them happy is if they believe they are the best and work their buttocks off. My concern is that they don't like themselves right now; they will come to appreciate themselves once they actually reach the age of majority when their mothers will enjoy them.

How much self-esteem do you have if you've had a rocky start in life and are currently living in squalor? Do you believe in your worth? You might also be suffering from a low sense of self-worth. However, there is a distinction between having low self-esteem and being plagued by a problem with self-esteem. Have you ever felt as if you didn't know who you were or where you belonged? Without a strong sense of self-worth, how can you know who you are?

If you're the parent of a child struggling with his or her self-esteem, you'll hear a lot of nonsense, something like "The problem is that they aren't putting forth sufficient effort. Their efforts must be increased." Really? What are you actually going to do when you get off the bench and they tell you that they aren't even trying to be competitive with themselves? Do you believe that they say this simply because they enjoy being a part of your group of friends? Think they've given it their all, do you believe that?

So, what is it about people who have been extremely bad and reached rock bottom? Does it makes them believe they are regaining their self-esteem? All this can be attributed to the fact that they are working extremely hard on their personal development. Schooling them, exposing them to new things, and allowing them to experiment with different ways of doing things are the effective way to boost their self-esteem. That is the primary factor in bringing about a shift in consciousness. You will see parents who have had a difficult start in life but have come out on the other side with their self-esteem and self-respect restored. These are people who are committed to their children and willing to put in the effort required.

Due to their desire to advance in their careers, they are probably spending a little more time in school than many of their peers. When you look at some of these kids, you'll notice that they aren't always hard at work. Instead of attending school, they are simply lounging on the front steps doing absolutely nothing. The majority of these individuals lack self-esteem. As a result of their failure to seek a better position in life, they have no self-respect whatsoever. They aren't attempting to attend school in any capacity. Simply put, they are using school as a social gathering place to meet new people.

So, what are their plans for the future once they graduate from high school? Not a great deal, I'm sure! Their ability to provide for themselves will be limited. In the end, they'll find themselves right back where they began. Their situation will necessitate a significant amount of assistance. Also, keep in mind that a significant number of children will have a high sense of self-worth as a result of hard work and dedication. In your opinion, what should be done about the people who have been good for the longest period? We all know how hard they've been working. Afterward, we inquire as to why they are continuing to engage in this practice. What do they have to say about it? "I don't actually know where else I could go right now. No other commitments exist for me right now." They have nowhere else to turn. Is it likely that they will withdraw? We don't think they'll go along with it, and the lack of self-esteem will be devastating in their lives. In addition, if they have any sense of self-worth, we won't be able to assist them when the time comes. I think the most serious issue with these children is that self-esteem is lacking in their lives.

Accepting your child's fears while also recognizing their accomplishments is critical in assisting your child in developing a healthy level of self-confidence. A child's ability to overcome their fear to achieve a goal is particularly noteworthy in this context, It is critical to remember that when working to increase a child's self-esteem, you must recognize and celebrate every small victory. Recognizing your child's accomplishments, no matter how small, will have a significant positive impact on them.

Recognize their accomplishments and empathize with their fears

When it comes to the process of instilling confidence in their child, parents must recognize that both are equally important factors. First, we will discuss the significance of praising a child's accomplishments as well as effective methods of doing so.

Recognize and Applaud Their Successes

Praise for your child's accomplishments, no matter how insignificant they may appear, is essential to the process of building confidence. This will make your child feel good about themselves and also help them to develop self-confidence because they will believe they are constantly doing things you find impressive.

Praise for your child's accomplishments can have a more positive outcome than constantly calling attention to the negative things your child may do. Constantly pointing out the wrong thing makes them believe that they are incapable of doing anything right. On the other hand, constantly praising your child's accomplishments and refusing to speak about their mistakes will have negative consequences as well. This is because the child will believe that they are incapable of doing anything wrong. Keeping a healthy balance between pointing out mistakes and praising accomplishments is critical for effective communication.

When you are praising your child's accomplishments, you must be careful not to spoil or overindulge him or her. If you give your child a substantial reward for every accomplishment, you can never go back to a small one or none at all. When they complete a small task, they will naturally come to believe that this will occur every time. When the rewards stop, the child may exhibit negative behavior because he or she will be perplexed as to actually why they are no longer receiving a reward for completing a particular task. It is recommended that larger rewards be saved for more significant achievements. Even a simple verbal commendation or a pat on the back will suffice when it comes to smaller accomplishments.

Recognize and Address Your Child's Fears:

Recognizing and addressing your child's fears can be extremely beneficial in the development of a child's self-confidence. You might be wondering how fear can help your child become more confident. When attempting to overcome fears, it is critical to first comprehend the situation. You don't want to put your child in a position of failure. Some of the things they may be apprehensive may be too difficult to complete. One of the worst things you can do is put them in a situation where they will not succeed. Talk to your child and find out what they are afraid of attempting. Then decide whether or not to encourage your child to face those fears head on.

Once you have gained an understanding of your child's fears and have determined the potential negative and positive consequences of confronting them, you can decide whether or not to motivate your child to do so. Accomplishing a task that a child had feared they would fail at is probably one of the most effective ways to help them develop self-esteem. The process demonstrates that they are capable of completing tasks, no matter how difficult or frightening they may appear to be if they put their minds to it.

You mustn't force your child to confront many fears at the same time. The result of pushing your child too hard might be something completely different from what you had hoped for. It may cause anxiety, which could hurt them for the rest of their life. This may serve to lower their self-confidence even further because the anxiety may prevent them from completing other tasks they were able to complete with ease.

Chapter 25
Learn to Accept Your Child for Who He or She Is

For the most part, accepting a child for who they are is not a difficult task for a parent. On the other hand, there are instances in which certain characteristics are extremely upsetting. This can be extremely detrimental to a child's sense of self-worth because their parents are supposed to be a constant source of approval and affection. There are some aspects of a child's personality they will never be able to change, and you will have to accept these aspects if you ever want your child to be happy with a high level of self-confidence.

Always remember that even though some of these things may be difficult for you to accept or may even go against your religious beliefs if you want your child to be confident and successful, you must accept them as well.

Accept your child for who they are, no matter what

Some aspects of your child's personality may be problematic, and you may wish they could be different. The reality is that your child will be unable to change certain aspects of their personality. You cannot hold your child responsible for who they are; they did not ask to be born into this world; you were the one who decided to provide them with life. Your child may engage in behaviors that you do not approve of, but you must accept them as a fact of life and devise a strategy for assisting the child in changing the behaviors in question.

Some examples of things your child cannot change about themselves:

Sexuality

This is most likely the area in which the greatest number of parents have difficulty accepting their child for who they are as a person. There are many reasons for this, including moral principles, religious backgrounds, and personal beliefs. Whatever the reason, you must learn to accept your child for who he or she truly is. When you demonstrate to your child that you accept and love them for who they are, they will experience a significant increase in self-confidence and feel much better about themselves. Apart from that, attempting to force your child to change something about themselves, such as their sexual orientation, will cause a child many difficulties in life. They will almost certainly become perplexed as to who they truly are, and this will undoubtedly hurt their future and confidence.

Favorite and least favorite things

You must learn to accept your child's likes, dislikes, and interests, as well as their differences. Understand that just because you want your son to grow up to be a football player or your daughter to grow up to be a beauty queen does not imply they want the same thing as you do. Although they may not follow your child's set dreams and goals, it is important to encourage them to pursue their own interests in life. Remember that it is their life, and they are the ones who must live it; parents are simply passengers on the journey who serve to guide them along the way.

Strengths and weaknesses of your child should be accepted

You must understand as a parent that your child may not be able to live up to all of your expectations at all times. Be realistic in your expectations of your child and be understanding when they are unable to meet one or more of them. If a child does not meet one of your expectations consistently, you will undermine the child's confidence and make them feel like a lesser person, unworthy of your time and attention. Demonstrating to your child that you will accept them as long as they put forth their best effort in everything they do will undoubtedly increase their self-confidence and help them lead a happier and more productive life. These are just a few examples of the countless characteristics of your child that you may have to accept one day.

Why Comparison is Unhelpful?

Comparison can be hard to avoid because it is the way we make sense of the world around us. When you start comparing your child to other kids, this causes jealousy. It can make them envious in a way that distracts them from what they should be focusing on such as school.

Stopping comparisons can be difficult because you're likely to be comparing yourself to other parents as well. The comparison trap is easy to fall into because that's how we make judgment calls. We often label ourselves as being "better" or "worse" than those we are comparing ourselves to. This should stop on all levels, and not just the way you compare your child. Circumstances are always going to be different for your child. If you take a similar situation and compare two parents, you could say that one did better and one did worse; but you may be disregarding many factors along the way.

Everybody's situation is going to be different because of the perspective we've been developing throughout our lives. The sooner you stop comparing, the sooner you will feel the relief from pressure that's been placed upon you and your child.

Creating Jealousy

Comparison can cause a child to feel self-doubt, so much so that they will question why they can't be like somebody else. They will look at what is deeply wrong with them, and they won't always be able to figure out the things that make them different. They will not believe they are good enough and will have this idea in their head that they are letting down and disappointing their parents. Comparison can lead to negative thoughts and instead of recognizing what they have, they focus on what everyone else does.

The jealousy will only continue to fester, and they might actively try to hurt the other person they are jealous of, even though they aren't even involved. A parent might always compare one child to their sibling, and that first sibling will take their jealousy out on the other brother or sister. This can cause them to have a strained relationship even though there wasn't any conflict in the first place.

Jealousy can also create hatred for the other person. Let's say that a parent is constantly comparing their child to the neighbor's child who might be getting good grades and have many successful accomplishments. They will grow jealous and start to feel hatred towards their parents. They will think their parents are not on their side and prefer their peers. This can cause turmoil and pain within the child's heart. It's important that we suspend this comparison to prevent negative feelings from growing within our kids.

Celebrating Your Child

As a parent, your number one job is to care for your child. This involves constantly celebrating them. Do everything you actually can in your power to make sure they know just how loved and how valuable they are. The first thing you can do is to allow them to be themselves. Take your child to their favorite place, let them pick out an outfit, or paint their room their favorite color. Buy them the things they want for their birthday and not just the things you want for them. Celebrate their individuality. Let your children do things for you. Give them the chance to help bake a cake. Let them frost a cupcake, even if it's disgusting and messy looking. Tell them how proud you are and how amazing they did something, even if it wasn't. Celebrate your child by giving them one-on-one time. Have dinner alone with them, take them to the movies or go shopping. Spend time alone with them at the park. Give them 100% of your attention, so they know they deserve to be celebrated.

Practice gratitude with your children. Let them know how grateful you are that they exist and all they have taught you. If they teach you something new, pretend to be extra excited and don't dismiss it as if you already knew. Let them share the information they have, even if it's something simple learned at school. Maybe they say something like, "Did you know chickens laid eggs?" Rather than saying, "Yes, I know, sweetie." Act thrilled that they just shared this new information. You don't have to lie; just say something like, "Wow, that's so cool!" You don't have to do it every time, but if you're constantly saying, "I know," to your child, it makes them feel less intelligent.

Let them pick out things for the overall home. Maybe you're going to buy some flowers; let them choose the ones they like, ask them what they want for dinner. They are not just people you are taking care of: they are an active part of the family, and they need to be treated as such.

Nourishing Originality

Children need to be nourished for their originality. You have to give them the freedom to be themselves. Let them think what they want and feel comfortable sharing when they feel insecure or confident. When you embrace a child's originality and celebrate with them, that alone will boost their confidence. It doesn't mean fitting them into a perfect mold of what they should be. You don't need to keep their hair brushed, have them wearing the nicest clothes and teach them to rephrase the perfect sayings over and over again. That will not breed confidence and, instead, it will put too much pressure on them. Celebrate their unique qualities and teach things that make them an individual.

Let them explore their creativity by giving them paints, blocks, and clay, and everything in between. They need to learn how to create, and you can encourage it. Of course, not all children are the next Picasso, but they might build interesting things with blocks or come up with incredible structures using clay. Teach your children to be respectful, but remember that there needs to be legitimate rules and restrictions in place; never just tell your child, "Because I said so." Sometimes that's the easiest way to explain something, but it creates confusing rules the child won't be able to follow. At the end of the day, your child is the only one who will ever be the way that they are now. Even if you have ten kids, each one is special in their own way. Don't compare them and do your best to suspend an ideal projection onto them. Celebrate all the things that make them their own person. They are deserving of this, and you should be nourishing that aspect as much as possible.

Chapter 26
How to Teach Your Kids to be Strong Mentally and Emotionally Balanced Kids

Figuring out how to raise an emotionally and mentally strong child is no easy task. Even if you want to nurture, support, and improve their mental well-being, parents will never be perfect in this area. That's why I've created a helpful checklist to guide you through what it takes to lead by example and give your child what they need emotionally and mentally.

How do you build a healthy emotional bond with your child?

The other night my husband and I had an amazing conversation with our 9-year-old son sparked by a game we play once a week. Every time we play, our conversations reach new depths, initiating discussions that wouldn't normally be easy to come by. This was a time in my parenthood when I realized that these conversations set the stage for our son's mental and emotional health with all the things of life. When you can have conversations like this with your kids, not just about "the conversation," but about what they're going to be going through in their lives, you'll prepare them that much more for emotional and mental success.

How to encourage your child to be emotionally strong?

Parenting depends on these conversations, no matter how awkward or difficult they may be at times because that's where you, as a parent, will be the most influential person in their lives. If you guide and don't control your children through parenting, it will cause them to trust your opinion and choose it over that of your friends or other potentially negative influences in your life.

A strong family bond creates an environment for your child where he feels safe and not judged. Where every question he or she has is not the wrong question but an ample opportunity to offer wisdom, guidance, and sound advice.

Stop thinking about "control" and start thinking about "acceptance".

Parenthood is not about control

As children reach their tweens and teens, you may need to step back and wait for them to come to you. If you want to give advice, be sure to ask him if it's okay. This will help them see that you are not trying to control them or control a situation, but that you are there to listen to them, understand them, and want them to be who they should be.

Educate them on the significance of appreciation

Not only can you be grateful for the things in your life, not complain and give generously, you can write it down in a gratitude journal. It can be done by boys and girls. Just print one at home! It is a great way for kids to be thankful for what they have and not dwell on what they don't have.

Teach them to apologize

The best way to teach this to your child is to apologize when you have wronged them. Also, if they are young, ask them to apologize if they hurt someone they are playing with or have offended. The earlier they learn this trait, the better.

Instruct them on the implication of giving and being generous

We live in a society where greed has taken over with a mindset that you have to put yourself first at the expense of others. Since I believe we need to teach our children to love and care for themselves and set boundaries, we also need to balance that with consideration for others.

In a world beset by consumerism and greed, we can teach our children about generosity and selflessness and the importance of giving our time, friendship, money, and service to others.

Teach them that not everything will work for them

Discipline is one of the best ways to teach your child that life won't always go his way.

Teach them that rejection and failure are part of life

My son struggles when he loses a game. He's super competitive (a big trait) but it often frustrates him when he loses, making him angry and then nobody wants to play him. I explained that failure, loss, or rejection will always be part of life. What matters most is what he actually does with it, and being happy for others when they win will help him overcome his frustration. To be honest, this is actually one of my son's biggest fights and I'll probably have to work with him for a long time to come.

When teaching these things to your children, it's important to remember that they don't always mean what you say when you say it. They are imperfect, so love them and accept them anyway. Carry on with them while they learn to do the right thing because more often than not you have to repeat yourself, remind them, and make them fail.

Knowing that you are there for them is often what will be remembered the most.

Chapter 27
Exercises for Making Friends

Human beings are innately social as we need other humans to survive. We enjoy spending time connecting with others and sharing our lives. Since the time we are babies, we look for connections, and this is how we remain safe and happy throughout our lives. For this reason, the development of conversational skills is very important to a person's overall social skills and his/her ability to make friends and connections with others. The more time your child spends talking to other people, the more he/she will develop and hone his/her communication and conversation skills. In this chapter, we will look at how you can help your child to develop his/her conversational skills.

Every single relationship requires a different style of communication. Just like how you wouldn't talk to your parents the same way that you talk to your best friend, you must always adjust your communication style based on the person you are interacting with. This is one concept that we will focus on when teaching children how to develop their conversational skills. Children are often unaware that they must adjust their communication style depending upon who they are addressing.

With Siblings or Friends

Friendship is when two people have a close association that is marked by feelings of respect, care, concern, admiration, and love. The main defining characteristic of a friendship can be simply described as a preference for a specific person. However, keep in mind that different people have their own definitions and requirements for friendship. For instance, young children may refer to someone as their "best friend" within the first five minutes of meeting them, but people from more reserved cultures or people who are shyer report having only had a few friends during their entire lives. For children, their siblings can be considered to be their best friends. Children are capable of having deep and loving friendships, just like adults.

In close friendships, we may express how we feel about the other person verbally by telling them that we enjoy their company and feel very comfortable being open emotionally with them. This is close to how we can communicate in familial relationships, but in friendships, we will speak in a more casual and joking manner.

When it comes to sibling relationships, these are often the closest friendships that your child will have. Since siblings live together and spend so much time enjoying activities, they are both friends and family at the same time. In these relationships, your child can feel more comfortable using a lot of nonverbal communication to show his/her siblings that he/she cares for him/her.

The touch barrier that often exists between friends or acquaintances will be broken, and your child will feel more comfortable showing his/her siblings how he/she feels and that he/she cares for them using nonverbal cues such as hugs or smiles. In these sibling relationships, they can also feel comfortable saying things like "I love you."

When teaching your child how he/she can better communicate with his/her siblings, it is important to remind him/her that he/she should make it a point to show his/her sibling(s) that he/she understands them and that he/she appreciates them. Siblings often fight, but the important thing is that they come back together as best friends at the end of the day. It is important to teach your child that for this reason, it is important for him/her to directly tell his/her siblings how much he/she appreciates them by saying things like "even though we fight, I appreciate having you as my best friend" or "I forgive you" and so on.

Practicing articulating his/her feelings in this way with his/her siblings is a great place to begin working on his/her conversational skills, as this is a place where he/she will often feel more comfortable sharing his/her feelings about how he/she feels about people. This will help him/her to practice being articulate, and this will help him/her in maintaining other relationships in his/her life, such as friendships or romantic relationships later on.

With Parents

The definition of family is "a fundamental social group in society, typically consisting of one or two parents and their children." However, you define family; all definitions of the word have one thing in common; family consists of the people who are very important to us in some way, thus identifying them as family. For children, the family is their most important group of relationships. Family is everything to a child, as it is where they learn and grow and are shown what love and care are. It is actually important for children to learn how best to communicate with their parents to have a healthy and happy familial relationship.

In familial relationships, we are often very comfortable with the people with whom we are interacting, such as our parents. With our family, we are often able to be ourselves and feel safe opening up emotionally. We can also usually read our family members quite well, and practicing empathy comes naturally. In these relationships, we often put aside things like insecurities and fears and be ourselves. Because of this, we do not need to spend much time wondering how we come across or how much eye contact we should give because we know that the lines of communication are open and if anyone is wondering what we mean, they will ask instead of remaining quiet and having a misunderstanding. This type of relationship is the first we form and is often the easiest type to conduct ourselves in, as we know these people will be with us no matter what.

When you are teaching your child about conversational skills when speaking to you, you will let him/her know that he/she can be comfortable and open with you and that you will listen to him/her no matter what he/she has to tell you. The most important thing you want to teach your child is that he/she can have open communication with you. This will become more and more beneficial as your child gets older, especially in his/her teen years. This is a time when he/she will be going through more and more challenges, and when having you as a confidant will become more and more important.

Activities for Developing Conversational Skills

One of the few best ways that you can help your child to develop his/her conversational skills is to have conversations with him/her as often as you can. You can do this at the dinner table while shopping with him/her at the grocery store while driving in the car with him/her and so on. The best way for kids to practice their conversational skills is to have as many conversations as possible. Conversations with adults will help them to speak with people who have a wider vocabulary, which will help them learn new words and the context in which to use them. In addition to this, you can play vocabulary games with your child to teach him/her new words, and then help him/her to think of different sentences that he/she can use these words in.

One fun activity that can help your child to develop his/her conversational skills is telling stories to bond with your child while also having him/her speak and explain himself/herself clearly and concisely. Sit in the dark together as a family, or just the two of you, and share ghost stories with each other. They can be either made up on the spot or stories that either you remember hearing before. When your child is a little bit older, he/she will be able to handle more scary ghost stories, and you can try to make up different stories to share with him/her. Try to encourage him/her to use harder and larger words as he/she gets older.

How Kids Can Make Friends

Making friends is something that all people need to do in life, as friends make life full and enjoyable. We all learn as children the best ways to make friends and keep them. There is evidence that shows that the kids who make friends the easiest are those who exhibit three specific traits:

Caring

Helping others

Sharing

Thus, to help your child to make friends, you will need to help him/her develop these traits. They are related to empathy and a child's impersonal skills.

Make Your Own Recycling Creations

This is a fun activity for children of all ages, especially parent-friendly, as it does not actually require much in terms of materials! Bring your recycling bin into your craft area or out into the backyard along with some tape, markers, stickers, and anything else your child could use to make his/her creation special. You can take part in this as well, or your children can do it on their own. They can get creative with the recycling bin by using old boxes and containers to build anything they can imagine. Some examples of creations that can be made easily are a robot, a city, an animal, a truck - or anything else at all! Encourage them to use as many items as possible from the recycling bin. The best part about this activity is that after your child has finished, you can put everything back into the bin with no mess and no extra garbage.

Music Crafts

Doing crafts with your child is a fun way to spend an afternoon, and it can be actually done by children of any age. Using a toilet paper or paper towel tube, take some small, dry pasta like macaroni or some small beads and fill the tube with them. Be careful that one of your children does not put these in his/her mouth, as it is a choking hazard for young children. Cover each end with paper or tissue and seal each end with an elastic band or tape. Then you are ready to decorate. Color and decorate your new musical instruments as you wish.

Once finished, you are ready to "shake, shake, shake," and able to make music together until your hearts are content! Babies can play music if it involves shaking, and they will enjoy hearing the sound of the shaking instruments you have made. Older children can have fun with the decoration and assembly portions of this craft, and they can even have fun trying to make sound patterns with their maracas in the end.

Balloon Volleyball

Outdoor volleyball can be played with many people, and it is just as much fun with two people as it is with ten people! All you need is a volleyball and something to use as a net. You can play your own game by bumping and volleying the ball back and forth and trying to get as many rallies as possible before the ball falls to the ground. This can be done with only two people if you want to play with your child, or they can play it with their friends.

If your child is younger, he/she can play this using a balloon instead of a volleyball. In this case, get on your knees and bounce the balloon into the air, having your child try to keep it in the air using his/her hands and arms. Try to get a rally going for as long as you can. Using a balloon will be safe and fun for little ones and older ones alike; and when he/she gets big enough, he/she will be able to join in on the fun with the real volleyball as well.

Have a Water Fight!

Playing with water guns is every child's dream. Playing with water guns with parent is an even bigger dream! If you offer to play with water guns with your child, it will be the happiest day of their life! Fill some water guns and run around outside with your child, spraying them and hiding behind trees or obstacles that you find along the way. You will both be laughing while also getting exercise and busting your boredom together!

Making Learnings their Ways of Life

Sometimes children have difficulty learning because they are not intelligent enough or because they do not recognize the benefits of learning a new skill. Assist them in recognizing and explaining the importance of learning. Consider turning learning about a new subject into an exciting opportunity for your child. You could explain that a large number of people are attempting to learn more about a specific topic. If you are interested in the learning, you'll get more out of the subject. It is possible to learn about it by reading a book or studying for a test.

Learning With the Help of Friends

One of the most and very effective methods of assisting your child in learning something new is to explain the topic to someone who will eventually become your child's friend (or vice versa). Kids usually enjoy learning with a friend, and they will frequently inquire about your friend's interests if you are willing to answer their questions. Allowing your child to go to a friend's house to learn allows him to meet new people.

Learning through Visualization

Additionally, to reading a book or watching a video, children learn through the visual representation of a concept. Consider presenting an idea through the use of a website or video. You could point out pictures and ask your child to look for specific details or common objects and items in the picture while you watch.

Learning with a Diagram

Using a diagram is another effective method of learning something new. iWeb.com, for example, can be used to create a diagram illustrating a specific subject matter. Using your computer, create a picture you can then print out and show to your child.

Learning in a Social Context

Even though children are constantly learning, they learn the most easily through social experiences. For example, a boy might be reading about a specific topic while playing with his brother in the backyard. While conversing with her friends, an older girl might read about a particular subject. Allow your child to interact with others!

Take steps to ensure that your child has something to do with friends at all times, whether it is actually playing games or working on art projects. It is also critical to assist your child in understanding the rules of the game when he is playing with others. Having to follow the rules will help him to learn more quickly and effectively. For example, if your child is participating in a game of "Capture the Flag," he or she will be required to actually adhere to the game's rules, which include maintaining a safe distance between teammates and moving quickly. He will actually learn more quickly if he is reminded to adhere to the rules regularly.

When children are interested in the topics being taught, they learn more effectively. In the case of birds, for example, when a child watches a video on the subject, she will know more about birds when she is asked to identify different birds in photographs. The most important thing is to encourage your child's interest in the material he is learning. If you are not interested in the subject, likely, your child will not be interested in it as well.

There are actually a plethora of educational resources available for children on the internet. The website www.allaboutlearning.org is a good place to start. Allaboutlearning.org also offers a free sample of learning guides for children, which parents can download. Parental resources can also be found on a variety of other websites. Myhomeworkhelp.com is a website where parents can get help with their children's schoolwork.

Find out how your child learns the most effectively. By understanding your child's learning style, you will better select the materials that will be most beneficial. By being aware of what your child is learning, you can make it easier for him to retain the information.

The amount of knowledge you have about the subject will determine how much your child learns. A child who has plenty of free time to learn will gain more knowledge than a child under pressure to complete his or her assignments. Learning is an extremely personal experience. Your child learns in a variety of ways and at different ages. Just as no single recipe is appropriate for every individual, no single method of instruction is appropriate for every child.

The creation of a learning environment is critical to the success of any new endeavor. If you want your child to learn, then you must teach him how to learn. If you are familiar with the subject matter, learning will be easier. To pique your child's interest in a subject, make certain that he has some involvement in the learning process. For example, allowing him to choose a topic, reading books or websites with him, or reading to him can all be simple ways to help.

Learning through Failure

Failure is something we want to avoid in life, but it can also be one of the most helpful teaching tools. Letting your kids make mistakes and have failures is very important as parents. You have to give them that opportunity to "mess up," so they know how not to in the same situation in the future.

Letting Them Fail

As a parent, a terrifying thing that you might not like to think about is the failure of your child. We want to do everything to try and prevent them from ever having to experience pain. Unfortunately, we will never be able to protect them from the hurt they will inevitably experience in life. It is up to us to make sure they are equipped with all the skills necessary so they can confront failure, overcome, and improve rather than let it destroy them. If you try to prevent your child from failing, it can make it even more challenging to try and fix a situation, which poses a challenge. There are a few things you can do to begin to make failure a little easier for both of you.

The first thing is to make sure that you let them make their own mistakes, even when you see a clear way to prevent it. Sometimes it is the only way a child will learn. Teaching our children how to do basic adult functions is something that parents are responsible for. Show them how to pour their glass of milk: they might spill it, but that's fine because you'll be there to clean it up. It might be messy for a moment, but you'll show them that mess ups aren't so bad. You just have to be ready to clean up a little after.

Of course, you'd never want to put your child in harm's way. But making mistakes is sometimes the only way to learn. Don't try to coach your child too much before certain things, either. Even something as simple as playing a game at the carnival, you want to let them go for it rather than trying to be perfect. Sometimes the child will get hung up on your demands and what you're saying, rather than trying to do things on their own. They might not make a mistake, but they also will not learn anything in the process.

Growth Mindset

There are two type, and you want to help make sure that your child is in a growth mindset. The other is to be avoided - a fixed mindset. A growth mindset is one filled with confidence. It lets the person know they are capable of doing anything they put their mind to. It encourages the individual to learn throughout life. A fixed mindset is involved with low self-esteem. The person might be too judgmental or critical of themselves. A growth mindset is one that embraces a challenge and gets excited about new opportunities. A fixed mindset is one that will always take the easy way out and avoid the slightest problem so they don't have to under anything too painful. Begin to focus on building a growth mindset for your child. You want to develop that confidence inside. There are a very few things you can do to make sure they're growing their mindset.

First and foremost, encourage them to try new and difficult things. Don't scare them away from something because they might fail. Let them know that even when they do fail, they are valid and worthy. Encourage them to accept risks and overcome the biggest mental challenges they may have to face. When you are praising and encouraging them, be specific about what you think they did well and let them know they were successful because they are intelligent.

Share ideas and tell them that they are safe. Remind them that success doesn't always mean that they are better or worse than anybody else. Don't limit their mindset. Let them know they can continually grow no matter what. If they don't know how to do something, let them know that they are capable of learning. Help them pursue that avenue if that is what they wish. Be persistent and don't give up on them, or else they will end up giving up on themselves.

Healthy Reflection

Reflection is an important part of growth. If you know how to reflect on yourself, then you will be able to look at issues and know how to overcome them. You can take your challenging thoughts and discover their root cause so you know how to overcome your limitations and negative mindset. You want to teach your child how they can healthfully reflect as well. You want to give them the tools necessary so they can look deep into their minds and discover the truth of the situation.

You can teach your child to reflect on themselves in many different ways. First, make sure you have one-on-one time where you can discuss this reflection. Begin with questions. Ask them about their day, not just what event they did, but what feelings and thoughts they had. Ask them what they enjoyed. Don't tell them how to feel but instead, lead them through the conversation so they bring up their own unique and organic thoughts and opinions. Encourage them to get deep into the things they are discussing. Ask them all of the W's of questions: who, what, where, when, and why. Don't overload or bombard them with questions to the point they become stressed. Refrain from talking too much: they should be doing the majority of the talking. Simply insert a comment when they need a push.

Let them spill every last detail to you without judgment. You can begin to include reflective activities, as well. Have them paint a picture or color a photograph of something they did in the past month or week. Tell them to write a story. Doing anything creative with your children helps them explore any feelings they had at that time. Look at pictures with your children. Show them when they were younger. Ask them what might have changed and what might have stayed the same. Remind them of how brave and intelligent they are now and how they have continued to grow. When you show your children that even if they are only five years old, they have grown, it reminds them that they are becoming a better and stronger person. You are teaching them to look back on themselves and notice any minor changes they went through. It's a healthy way to promote growth in children.

I am Confident and Self-reliant

Confidence comes from positive outcomes. Positive outcomes fuel confidence and serve as motivators, helping kids improve. When something they did reaps a positive outcome, they feel more confident and self-reliant. When they feel confident and assured, they feel empowered to invest their time and resources in other things too. Confidence is what makes kids persistent. Without it, they give up soon or simply don't start at all. We can say that it is what saves kids from despair and hopelessness.

Barriers to Self-confidence in Kids

However, there are some barriers when encouraging kids to be self-confident. Before we head straight into teaching you strategies to help empower your kids to become confident adults, it is only fair to know of and eliminate the factors that pose hurdles in our efforts.

Self-Defeating Assumptions

Some kids just think that they can't, so they don't try. Sometimes, they become so rattled by a little inconvenience that they call it quits to the next one without even a single attempt. They decide to let go of something, assuming they won't be able to have it. For instance, a child may decide to learn to play baseball. However, every time they try to play catch with their older sibling, they miss all catches. So, they decide to not join the school team—assuming they will be bad at it. These are what we call, self-defeating assumptions. It's good to be realistic, but that doesn't mean you start to act like a loser before even trying. Kids who believe in such self-defeating assumptions can be hard to train.

Setting Unrealistic Goals

On the contrary, some kids act like big shows and take up more than they could handle. It's ambitious to tackle BHAGs (big hairy audacious goals) but only if you are prepared for it. Enormous goals often undermine confidence. This can stem from demotivation and depression. Confidence is something that mostly comes from small wins at first.

Celebrating Too Soon

Do you have a child who celebrates their weight loss by eating an entire cake? What kind of celebration is that? Kids who claim to be victors before reaching their end goals can trigger a lack of confidence when they fail at the next stage. For instance, your kid scores high grades in math during a class test. They confidently announce it to the whole class that they will be one getting the highest grade in math in the finals. Seems the right kind of anticipation? But before the finals, they have to score high in the next test too, which they don't. And then there goes their confidence out of the door.

Blaming Others

Kids who don't own up to their mistakes and instead blame others for their mishaps are also hard to train. They, themselves are the barrier to building confidence as they aren't willing to listen and make amends for their behavior and thoughts. Even when wronged by someone, we still have the choice to either cry about it or make a difference for ourselves. Sadly, kids who choose the first often report having poor confidence and show resistance when schooled about it.

Not Anticipating Setbacks

A child who doesn't anticipate setbacks and moves forward with blind optimism may stumble and fall hard on their head. Optimism is a good thing but when it clouds the mind of a child, they forget about the dangers and challenges along the way. Therefore, when something unexpected happens, they lose their confidence and edge. This is the hardest to treat as they have had a taste of positivity before and now have turned bitter and hopeless.

Being Overconfident

There is a very delicate line between being confident and arrogant, and children who aren't aware of this frequently find themselves on the wrong side. Arrogance can lead to neglecting the basics, turning a deaf ear to critics, and being blinded by the forces of change.

Learning to Shut the Inner Voice

All kids need positive affirmations to defeat the inner critic. As parents, we can help them find that positivity and turn their negative perceptions into something positive and progressive. First, we must use language that reeks of positivity, even when they feel down. This kind of outlook about everything is what they are going to pick up and use to uplift their confidence.

You must, at all times, love them. This seems rather debatable as every parent thinks they love their child unconditionally. True, but sometimes we forget to show it. Love demands actions and actions drive behavior. Dole out plenty of love their way to encourage and make them realize that they always have an actual strong support system behind them. This means putting an end to baseless comparisons and extremely high expectations that they will fail to meet. Every child, including yours, needs to feel accepted and looked after. When we yell, shout, or ignore them, we are unconsciously undermining their level of confidence. Ever had your child actually come up to you to show you how well they have colored the drawing? They are attention-seekers naturally and when they don't get that, "Wow, this looks amazing. Let's hang it on the fridge for your daddy to see," they lose their confidence.

This takes us to the second important practice: praising them when it's due. Holding back praise is another reason why some kids suffer from a lack of confidence. Positive feedback, even for adults, is essential. So why deprive our kids of it? Praise them even if they have repeated the same practice for the hundredth time. Wat you don't know is that when they feel encouraged and praised, they try to do it better than the last time. Praise can also result in repeated actions, the perfect way to develop new habits such as persistence, resilience, and improved confidence.

Speaking of resilience, your child must also be taught that success isn't always a guarantee. There is a chance of setbacks and unexpected failures and pain. They must know how to overcome and cope with such hardships without losing their confidence. Teaching resilience means we promote moving forward and not dwelling on the failures for too long.

Next, you must at all times and by all means, foster a growth mindset. Unlike a fixed mindset that suggests that humans are born with all the talents and skills they will ever possess, a growth mindset strongly believes in the possibility of learning new skills and cultivating talents over time. This is the kind of mindset you need your child to have.

Another way to build confidence is to help the child pursue their passions. It is a no-secret secret that everyone acts more driven and passionate when it comes to doing something they love. Say, your child loves to draw. If you encourage them to follow their passion and improve their skills, they will feel more confident.

And finally, while helping them build confidence, don't forget to set goals that are achievable and tell them what is expected. Set uncomplicated rules they can follow easily and don't be too hard on them when they fail to follow them. The goal shouldn't be to enforce rules and be strict but to help them work around any setbacks and offer more clarity. When they know what is expected of them and how to get there, they will feel more confident.

Time to Toughen Up!

Most of these strategies are backed by years of experiments and research studies, a testament of how productive they are.

Try Strength-Based Parenting

According to Lea Waters, a professor at the University of Melbourne, strength-based parenting focuses on the identification and cultivation of positive states, qualities of your child, and processes they go through when faced with a certain situation. Think of it as an addition of a positive filter on parenting that aids parents in teaching kids how to react to stress. This eliminates the chance(s) of kids using aggressive coping reactions or complete avoidance to run away from a stressful situation.

During a preliminary study, Walter and her colleagues explored this newfound concept with a group of primary-school-age children in Australia's middle schools (Waters, 2015). The participating kids were presented with a stressful scenario such as breaking up with a friend over some small fight or being the only student in the class to not have completed an assignment due the next day. The kids were asked to discuss their responses. The majority of the kids came up with negative responses such as freaking out, being depressed, or getting angry. Only a handful listed positive means to cope with the proposed situation. They came up with responses like breathing techniques to get over something faster and reminding themselves of all the good times they had actually spent with that friend. They also indicated their parents appreciated their strengths and encouraged them to use these kinds of techniques in times of stress to deal with it better.

This suggests that parents who focus more on the skills and strengths of their children rather than pulling them down for their weaknesses are also those who teach them to cope better with stress.

Problem-Solve with Them

Not many parents are aware of the fact that their words hold immense value in the way kids express themselves. If they are reluctant and less open to communication, kids will refrain from coming to them to discuss how they are feeling. As a result, they may take up unhealthy coping strategies and cause further harm to themselves in the future. Therefore, be communicative and offer problem-solving ideas. Encourage them to actually think of ways to overcome a certain situation or challenge instead of telling them what to do exactly. Some responses can be:

What do you think we should do right now?

Can you tell me how I can make you feel better right now?

When you faced a similar situation before, what worked for you?

Can you fill me in with what is going inside your head?

What can you do to get out of this mess?

Notice how none of these statements offers solutions but rather encourage your kid to come up with one on their own.

Introduce Self-Discipline

Remember the ever-so-famous marshmallow effect? Here's a little reminder if you aren't able to recall the years old test for delayed gratification and self-discipline. Psychologist Walter Mischel called in a few kindergarteners for a test that involved marshmallows. In front of them, each child had a plate containing one marshmallow. The researcher was then called in by someone (planned) but before leaving the room, the researcher made a simple request. If the child wanted, they could have the marshmallow right away, but if they waited for the researcher to come back, they will have two. The request was simple but portrayed something very deep within us. It showed how we all are prisoners of instant gratification. Many kids ate the marshmallow without waiting for the researcher. But those who didn't and showed remarkable self-discipline even at such an early age went on to have greater academic scores, better careers, and healthier relationships than their counterparts.

Coming back to the point, every parent must teach their children principles of self-discipline so they learn to behave appropriately, even when overwhelmed by emotions. The best way to teach a kid is to make them understand the perks of distraction from temptations. Surely, you may feel like crying a river in the supermarket because the store is out of your favorite gummy bears, but you have to behave and act better. This also builds resilience.

Allow Them to Take Calculated Risks

Be clear when telling them their courage and willingness to fight back and manage emotions is far more commendable than the outcome they achieve. Help them find their freedom to make choices and take decisions so even when they make mistakes, they have no one to blame but themselves. Freedom will facilitate them in knowing what their triggers are, how they can navigate their emotions better, and how to cope with the things that aren't in one's control. They should always be encouraged to take risks and try new things so when they fail, they learn to get over it and move on. If they won't try anything new, they will spend their whole life in a predictable manner and lose their calm the minute something odd happens. Therefore, it is better to prepare them for uncertainty beforehand.

Avoid Shielding them from Stress

According to Dennis Charney, a psychiatrist at the Icahn School of Medicine, children who have been through some traumatic experience in their life such as the loss of a parent or loved one, suffered domestic assault, been hit by some natural disaster or been jailed, do better than those who hasn't been through something like that. They portray improved coping skills in difficult times as opposed to those who have had things handed to them with ease.

She explained why such kids are better at bouncing back and healing faster. She believes that since kids who have been through some traumatic incidents have faced challenges right in their faces instead of avoiding their existence or reality, they emerged stronger. For parents, this means engaging kids in challenging tasks, so they learn to cope better and make sense of what is happening instead of running in the other direction. But don't get us wrong, this doesn't mean leaving them in a forest to find their way back home or in an empty parking lot. It is about exposing them to controlled stressful situations that makes them come up with a plan to get out of them. When kids are left on their own to deal with their problems, they develop a psychological toolbox of coping strategies that come in handy when they are adults.

Foster Optimism

Research suggests that optimism is one of the chief traits of resilient people (Ong, et al., 2006). They see the grass greener on both sides, know that the glass is filled (not half-filled or half-empty), and live with a positive outlook towards life. Optimism kills stress and we don't need to provide you with facts to convince you. Therefore, as parents, you must try to nurture optimism by exposing your kids to experiences that make them happier. This doesn't mean you go on invalidating the way they feel but rather presenting them with opportunities that makes them see life as beautiful and worthy. To help them cope with an existing emotion, try to find something positive in it. For example, if your child had been planning for weeks for a school trip and for some reason it got canceled at the last minute, take them someplace they enjoy going to so they understand that all is never lost.

The idea is to refocus their attention on what is left from what has been lost.

Increase Social Interactions

Social support is another great way to build resilience and grit in children. When kids are surrounded by people who admire, encourage, and support them through thick and thin, they feel loved and looked after. Social support has been linked to positive emotions, predictable behavior, and improved self-esteem, motivation, and personal control. It comes from those who always cheer them on when they are faced with difficult emotions. Strong connections with people who love them also make them resilient.

Tell Them it is Okay to Seek Help

Being brave doesn't always mean dealing with things alone. It also means you can seek assistance when required without feeling ashamed or guilty. After all, two minds are always better than one, so remind them to seek help and not carry all the burdens alone.

Let Them Heal

Often, we presume that resilience is about never failing. But it is about getting back up, recovering, and gaining control of your life. A lot of times, parents try to rush through an array of emotions, hoping the sooner their system is flushed off them the better. But like any injury, a broken or hurt person needs time to heal. There is a reason why we feel things so deeply. We can't push them away or get over them in a minute. This is deceit and denial, and sooner or later, they will crawl back into our minds and do the damage. The healing time comes when one reviews the problem, reflects upon and processes mistakes, and finds means to restore balance. Rushing through emotions doesn't build resilience; embracing and acknowledging them does!

Creating Dreams

Children are individuals. Though they don't seem like it now, one day they will be adults that have to make their own decisions. It's essential we equip them with that capability for years to come. Before your children were born, you might have had a vision for what you hoped they would become. As parents, we all would love our children to grow up to be successful, happy, independent, and healthy. Some parents have a different view of what this means from their children.

A parent might hope their kid grows up to be a successful doctor. That child might hate anything related to math or science, and instead, they become a painter. That can seem especially disappointing to the parent because they had an expectation for their child already. They might still believe well into adulthood of their children that they know best for their child, when really that kid is doing exactly what they should be to make them happy.

This type of parent won't always realize that it's not the child who is disappointing them, but that their unfulfilled vision of the future, which can be confusing and scary. We all have expectations; and when things go differently than what we predicted, it can feel as though we are being let down. It can be nerve-wracking to let your child be independent. You have to suspend some of the control you had when they were younger. The older a child gets, the less power we have over their actions. However, a child never stops needing their parents. They will always go first to you for advice, and that's the way it should be.

Parents are teachers, therapists, role models, coaches, instructors, and everything in between; but they are not guards, bosses, controllers, or rulers. You don't want to push your child away; instead, you want to guide them through major life decisions. They won't always decide to do what you want them to do, but that's a good thing! You should be really proud of your child if they are making their own decisions in an independent way. It shows great parenting, as opposed to a form where you are controlling their every last move, making them feel bad about not choosing the things that you want for them, and so on.

Parental Projection

As a parent, it's vital to recognize what you might be projecting onto your child. Projecting means you are taking your own experiences and placing them on this other individual. That's incredibly hard not to do because our childhood affects how we parent. The way you were treated when raised can sometimes bleed into what you do for your child.

The first thing you might notice, once you become a parent, is that you begin to imitate your parents. Perhaps you have never had a problem managing your anger, but then all of a sudden, once your child does something wrong, you snap and lash out. This might be triggered by something that reminds you of your childhood. Maybe you were trying to pour yourself a glass of juice and it spilled all over the floor, so your dad yelled at you. Then, when your child does the same thing, you might be triggered into that same reaction without even fully realizing it. Your brain has been normalized to think that way. You lash out and then suddenly realize that you were acting like your parents. This can hurt your inner critical voice, and it can shame your child and destroy their confidence.

It can be hard once we become parents to look back and criticize our own. We make mistakes, and so surely they are allowed to have made their own mistakes too. Unfortunately, that doesn't mean they didn't still hurt us at times. Instead of normalizing that behavior, we have to do our best to overcome it as we parent our children. You might also notice that you are projecting the things you want for your child onto them. Maybe your parents were strict, so now you give your child too much freedom in an attempt to overcome it.

Children are extensions of ourselves in a sense, but we should strive to remember that they are autonomous individuals completely different from us. Another projection is to see their children as they saw themselves when they were children. Perhaps a parent was a troublemaker in school, always getting yelled at by their parents. Now they have a child and when he or she acts out, the parent refers to this child as a troublemaker because they associate it with how they were viewed. We have to do our best to separate our perspective of who we are from our perspective of our children.

Sometimes, as parents, we might become defensive and closed off in certain situations. As a child, you might have been yelled at or punished too often, to the point that you created a defense and a brick wall on your emotions to protect yourself. This was a way for you to survive as a child, but as an adult, it can lead to you alienating people and shutting feelings off. You have to recognize that what happened in your childhood affects you now so that you can avoid projecting yourself onto your children. Children do not exist to heal their parents. They are opposite individuals and need to be treated as such.

Coaching Versus Controlling

Children will always need guidance, even when they start having families of their own. It's actually important that we do our best to coach them along the way, rather than trying to control all the actions that they have. The first thing you have to do is recognize the child's individual needs. Some children learn better when told what to do and then given a chance to try. Other children only learn as they do the task with you. Some children prefer to teach themselves and have supervision after the fact. Become aware of your child's learning style so you can make sure you are adhering to their individual needs.

Remember that their emotions can sometimes bring you closer. Even if they seem upset, you don't always have to tell them to stop expressing those emotions. Instead, you can help develop those feelings and teach them to talk about them in a healthy way. Make sure you understand the limits and boundaries you have to set to provide your children with the proper structure. Every time you want to give them a command, think if it could be stated as a question. For example, rather than saying,

"Don't do that, that's not a good idea," you can instead ask, "Have you really thought out all of the consequences?" When you ask this question, you are forcing them to think about it, and they will have to answer for themselves. When you tell them a command, you are putting that command in their mind, and then they can choose whether or not to follow it. They can actively do the opposite to show defiance, or they can absorb all your commands and become incapable of making their own healthy decisions. Guide them. Don't push. Gently sway them into a pattern of explorative thinking, rather than pulling them by a string along the path of your thoughts.

Encouragement

Anything you will ever do as a parent should involve positively encouraging your child. You want to always, always, always show that you are proud of them and persuade them to actually continue on the same path of healthy encouragement. When you do this, you are giving them the chance to create their own healthy life.

The first encouragement is to show them that they are loved as much as possible. When a child feels loved, they know that they are worthy and valued. You remind them that even though they make mistakes and have flaws, you will always be there at the end of the day to provide compassion. Remind your children that you trust them and know they are intelligent. Let them know you have faith in their decisions and that they are strong enough to handle it. Children need to know that even though they might not be able to make as big of an impact as others, they still have power to change the world.

They are still a valuable asset to your home, community, and the world in general. Remind your child that they have worth. When you give them a purpose and something to live for, they will fight to protect it. If you never encourage them and don't instill the belief that they are capable, they will never achieve what they are meant to. Remind them that their emotions are valid and it is okay for them to feel the way that they do. They are completely justified in all the thoughts and feelings they have. Let them know that they can have choices. They are in control of their actions and the ones who decide what is good and what is bad. Remind them that they are growing. They are patient, strong, brave, valuable, beautiful, interesting, and good. The more you remind them of these positive qualities, the more they will believe them. When a child truly believes these encouraging things, they will achieve true confidence. Children do not learn through shaming: they are not taught how to think positively when they're only fed negativity.

Sometimes harsh things can be motivators. Maybe somebody was upset because you weren't able to go out to a fancy restaurant with them, which motivated you to save your money. Perhaps somebody commented on not knowing enough about history, so you decided to start reading more books. Sometimes negative encouragement pushes you in the right direction because we adults, we are capable of creating our own thoughts. Children are still learning how to even think in the first place. When they are only fed negativity, they will only create negativity in their minds. Remind them that even when somebody may say something against them or offer criticism, they are greater than the words given. They are important and have great ideas. Even when they might make mistakes, they will always be worthy of love and compassion.

Chapter 28
Psychology Tricks to Build Resilience and Unstoppable Confidence in Children

While some people crash under the pressure of adversity and fight hard to recover, others are able to do so quite fast from even the most catastrophic of traumas and difficulties. Psychological resilience is indisputably essential in life; it helps you face the ups and downs of existence. When something good happens, it helps you to enjoy it without the fear of losing it, without thinking that you don't deserve it, or without the fear of what will come next. When something bad happens, it helps you not to lose yourself, not to crash completely, and not to be completely broken. It reminds you that it is always possible to find a solution, and even if there is no solution, to just keep going on. Psychologists are interested in understanding psychological resilience and how to develop it - particularly in children.

We all wish we could shield our children from the stress that comes with living in an uncertain time and the negative influence that social alienation has. We wish we could protect them from everything. Unfortunately, some conditions are beyond our ability to control. However, we can influence the lessons kids take away from bad experiences. In life, resilience is the ability to cope and bounce back from obstacles that come our way. It may make the difference between being able to handle pressure and losing your cool under pressure. People who are more resilient tend to have a more optimistic attitude on life and are better at dealing with stress. Research shows that although some individuals seem to be born with resilience, these characteristics may also be learned. The question is how?

Unpleasant feelings shouldn't be avoided or repressed; rather, we must allow ourselves to confront difficult emotions to go forward. Not dealing with bad feelings can be dangerous. The bad energy does not disappear; it stays with you, makes your spirit heavier, and one day it will explode, causing even more damage.

The first thing is admit there is a problem, that you are going through something difficult and it is okay to feel bad about the situation. Keep in mind that life can get hard without a particular reason, so don't think that the universe is against you or it is your fault. It is important to consider if you could have done something that led you in the situation or how to make it better. After those considerations, your time to think about the past is over, and now you have to fight for the future.

Being strong and resilient is very personal; you have to find out what works for you and makes you feel a little better (even just a little is a good start). You can make a list and try certain activities on different days. Rate them on a scale from one to ten, so at the end of each of the week you can see what is working better for you and improve the other activities.

An example of activities:

Read a book

Listen to music

Sing

Bake a cake

Meet a friend

Take a nap

Have a walk

Run

Write a story or a diary

Draw something

Try painting

Do some shopping

Watch a movie

Make some gifts (maybe handmade ones)

Dance

Learn how to play an instrument

Learn something new

Teach those same things to your kids. Even young ones experience hard times and feel anxious or depressed. Tell them that it is normal and that everything is going to be alright. Let them deal with the feelings and cry if they feel so inclined, but establish some point in which you two together start to fight back. Help your kids with the list of activities and make sure to listen to their suggestions to see what is working. You are transforming the bad energy to improve even more.

You alone are responsible for your own level of adaptability and resilience. Despite the fact that you may be confronted with a variety of obstacles entirely beyond your control, every situation can be used to build something new. See obstacles as a challenge, something that allows you to show yourself how strong and resilient you are. Try to explain to your kid using a metaphor. Tell them that every superhero has something to fight and it is just by fighting that they discover their own superpowers.

By responding to adversity in a healthy way, we strengthen our potential to be resilient over time. Alternatively, even when life delivers us lemons, we may practice making lemonade! And the term "practice" is the most vital one to remember in this context. Resilience is a skill that can be learned, not a personality trait that can be gained or lost.

This is reassuring news since it means you have control on your degree of adaptability and resilience. Coping with challenging circumstances is a necessary part of learning how to be strong and resilient; otherwise, you will never master these skills.

Children must have confidence in their own abilities; but also remember that they will be able to deal with it if unsuccessful. Children develop a healthy self-confidence as a result of experiences with failure and how they were able to fight back even if it was hard for them! The fact that you tackle new occupations with a positive attitude and rigorous preparation is a fantastic model for youngsters to emulate. Diversifying their interests is advantageous for youngsters, rather than putting all their energy on a single activity. Just because your kid is good at sports, for example, doesn't mean that he or she shouldn't try intellectual activities too! Learning new skills allows youngsters to feel more confident in coping with whatever challenges come their way. Although it is normal to want to protect your kid from failure, children learn via trial and error, and falling short of a goal helps them realize that failure is not necessarily a death sentence.

It may push youngsters to put up more effort, which will be helpful to them as adults. Developing the ability to endure in the face of adversity, rather than giving up after a single setback, is a critical life lesson. While being the best at everything all the time is important for building confidence and self-esteem, it is also important to be resilient enough to keep trying and not become dejected when you are unsuccessful.

Acknowledging and achieving goals, no matter how large or small, helps youngsters feel more in control of their lives. Encourage your child to make a list of things they want to achieve to assist them in turning their aspirations and desires into feasible goals. Then consider breaking down longer-term goals into smaller, more doable benchmarks. You will be validating their interests while also supporting them in building the qualities they will need to reach their goals throughout life.

Recognizing and applauding children for their accomplishments is important; but, expressing gratitude for their efforts regardless of the outcome is even more important. Learning new skills requires a significant amount of work, and the results are not always immediately apparent. Express to youngsters your appreciation for the work they are putting in, whether they are newborns building with blocks or teenagers learning to play the guitar for the very first time. Children should be encouraged to complete age-appropriate chores like picking up toys or washing dishes to feel more connected to their families and more respected by their parents.

Children benefit from challenges, but they should also be given opportunities in which they become be certain of reaching success, according to experts. Activities that will make your child feel comfortable and secure enough to embark on a harder activity should be encouraged. Communicate to your child that you will always appreciate him or her no matter what happens. It doesn't matter whether you win or you lose the big game, if you receive good grades or bad grades. This is true even if you are angry with him at the moment.

I believe it is critical to communicate to your child that you believe they are good and loved all of the time, not only when they do big things. This will assist them in feeling better about themselves even when they aren't feeling good about themselves at the time. Perfection doesn't exist, and it is vital that children learn this lesson as soon as possible.

Youngsters believe that others are always happy and successful, dressed immaculately and this is a misconception that may be harmful their mental well-being. Inform them that being anything less than perfect is quite normal and fully acceptable to you.

Competence

Competence is defined as the capacity to deal with a variety of circumstances successfully. It is not only a hazy sense of confidence that "I can accomplish this." Children gain competence when they learn abilities that enable them to put their confidence in their own judgement and make responsible decisions.

When we recognize and celebrate the accomplishments of young people while simultaneously providing them the opportunity to learn new skills, they feel empowered. When we discourage young people from attempting something new—and from coping on their own if they fail—we are undermining their ability to be competent. Encourage youngsters to concentrate on their strengths and build on them.

Whenever they successfully manage a problem, they should recognize what they have done well and how their actions benefit others and them. Allowing children to make safe errors gives them the chance to learn from their mistakes. Avoid the temptation to shield them from every stumbling block. For small children, lectures are too complicated, while for adolescents, they are too stressful to hear and comprehend in full. Break down concepts one step at a time instead so that they can properly comprehend your remarks.

Contribution

When youngsters discover that the world is a better place because they are a part of it, it is a tremendous realization. They have a feeling of purpose as a result of realizing the significance of their efforts, which might inspire them to take action to make the world a better place someday. Giving back feels good and is motivated by dedication and duty rather than pity. This allows children to feel more comfortable asking for help from others without feeling embarrassed or ashamed.

Children (of suitable age levels) should be made aware that many individuals across the globe do not have access to as much money, freedom, and security as they need. Instill the importance of helping others in your children. Generosity of your time, energy, and resources should be modeled. Create chances for youngsters to make a particular contribution, such as via volunteer work.

Connection

In a child's existence, one of the most protecting factors is the unconditional love you provide. Understanding and empathizing with children's good and negative emotions makes them feel recognized, understood, and appreciated. This emotional safety net provides children with the foundation they need to express their emotions and find out answers to their difficulties. Connections to civic, educational, religious, and sports organizations may also help young people feel more at home and secure in their surroundings.

Allowing children to experience and express a wide range of emotions is important. Don't give them any reasons to repress their negative emotions. Demonstrate that interpersonal connections are important by confronting disagreement head-on. Instead of allowing issues to fester, try to find a solution to them. Encourage your children to form deep bonds with their peers and adults. Set a good example by cultivating healthy connections in your own life.

Character

Every family has its own definition of what it means to be of good moral character. Whatever the circumstances, children need a basic understanding of right and wrong to be prepared to contribute to the world and grow up to be responsible individuals. This is what character is all about. It assists youngsters in being more confident in their ideals and exhibiting a caring attitude toward others as they grow older. Talk to your children about how their actions influence other people, both positively and negatively. When making decisions, encourage youngsters to think about what is right and what is wrong. Assist them in seeing beyond their immediate needs or self-centered aspirations.

When making judgments or taking actions, say out loud how you consider the needs of others in your decisions or activities. Working with youngsters to explain and communicate their own beliefs is a worthwhile endeavor. Be a role model. Your deeds are more persuasive than your words.

Confidence

Confidence is a firm conviction in one's own talents and abilities. It is not created by telling children that they are exceptional or valuable. Instead, when they exhibit their skills in real-life settings, youngsters acquire confidence in themselves. As a result of their parents' encouragement and support, they think they are capable of dealing with obstacles and gain the confidence to attempt new things.

They have faith in their capacity to make wise decisions. Place more emphasis on the development of character values such as justice, honesty, perseverance, and kindness rather than only on academic accomplishments. Children need to be recognized and praised in an honest and particular manner. Instead of saying "You're a fantastic artist!" use something like "I really like the colors you chose in that picture." Specific praise is more credible, and your criticism will have a greater effect if it is specific.

Coping

Children who learn to manage stress efficiently will be better equipped to face the difficulties of life in the future. Kids who are able to discern between a catastrophe and a relatively modest setback will be less anxious and experience less stress overall. A diverse repertoire of good, adaptive coping methods may also assist children in avoiding the use of potentially harmful fast solutions for stress.

When people are in a state of crisis, methods such as exercising, relaxing, practicing relaxation techniques, sleeping and eating properly might help them feel more comfortable and hopefully release some stress. Teach your youngsters to analyze the situation in an objective way so they will be able to tell the difference between a genuine crisis and something that seems to be a crisis at the moment. Demonstrate how to solve problems step by step.

Control

When children's choices have an impact on their lives, they learn that they are in command of their destinies and they have what it takes to bounce back after adversity. In a situation where parents control all the decisions, children may assume that things happen to them rather than realize that things happen because of their actions. Children who lack a feeling of control may believe that their activities are insignificant. They may become quiet, cynical, or even sad as a result. Children who are resilient, on the other hand, are aware they have internal control.

They are well aware that they can make a difference. Encourage youngsters to celebrate even the smallest of victories so they see that they can achieve their goals. It does not have to be a big and fancy celebration: some words and a hug are enough. Increased independence should be given as a reward for accountability. It's important to remember that the term "discipline" refers to the act of instructing rather than punishing or controlling.

Chapter 29
Life Skills to Start Teaching Your Child at Very Early Age for Fortune

Management of your Time

When it comes to keeping your family organized, time management is essential. In addition, children should be taught time management skills as early as possible. You may make your days easier if you teach younger children how to manage time, remain on task, and establish a routine. When people learn to master time management, they can do anything from getting up on time in the morning to arriving at their job in the morning.

Food Prep

Even the tiniest of eaters can learn to cook a meal. Preschool and primary school students can be taught how to make a sandwich, and you can also teach them how to operate a microwave. In addition, your children can serve as your sous chefs when you're in the kitchen. Learning how to bag their lunch, make healthy food choices, cook on the stove with adult supervision, and plan their meals are some additional life skills that your children can learn as they get more comfortable in the kitchen.

Management of Financial Resources

Our children are taught to count. Our children are taught the fundamentals of math. It's possible to turn such lessons into life skills that students can use right away. Many folks have a hard time managing their finances. To assist your children in becoming financially savvy, teach them about money, its value, and how to work it properly. To help your children learn how to save, spend sensibly, and make the change, teach them good money management. Since using checks, credit cards, and cash apps isn't free money, they must understand this.

Cleaning

It's sometimes easier for parents to take care of all the housework. This is a missed opportunity to teach our children about housekeeping, so when they leave home, they know how to take care of their place: how to make a bed, empty the dishwasher, and dust furnishings. Consider the messes your children produce regularly and how they can help clean them up. Keep a sponge or towel in the bathroom so that youngsters may clean up the toothpaste globs they leave on the counter. Throw all the kids' toys into a basket so they put them away at the end of the day when they've been moved from room to room by magic.

Keeping Up with the Housework

Kids are often eager to help around the house; there is always some basic upkeep that they can assist with. Start with simple activities like teaching children how to change the toilet paper rolls or put away the garbage bags. As youngsters grow older, they can learn how to change a light bulb, unclog a drain, and replace the vacuum cleaner bag independently.

Putting on the Clothes and Getting Ready

Children might begin to learn how to prepare themselves at a young age. Before they go to sleep, let them choose their outfit for the next day. Make sure they can easily set the alarm on your alarm clock. Set out their brushes and toothpaste. The entire procedure should be illustrated via pictures. Please take a photo of their alarm clock, their clothes, an image of their toothbrush, their hairbrush, and even the toilet to remind them to use it before leaving the house. These photos serve as daily flashcards until children develop the habit of preparing themselves independently.

Skills in Making Decisions

Every youngster should learn how to make wise judgments at an early age. Choosing chocolate and vanilla ice cream, blue and white stockings, and playing trains and automobiles are your first options. Learning about the benefits and repercussions of good and bad decisions can begin in elementary school. It would be best if you walked through your child's decision-making process, then watch how things turn out after you've helped them consider their options and weigh the benefits and drawbacks of each.

Make the Most of your Love and Manage your Stress

Father and Mother need to take care of them because their children are sensitive to stress. Young children cannot be over loved or overly affectionate. Long-term success is more likely to be attained when children feel safe. Sing, dance, and point to an object while talking. It helps the child learn to correlate words with specific things. Before the ability to speak, some infants can point.

Count, Group, and Compare

This tip is about math skills. Studies have shown that babies are naturally good at math. Children can be taught math vocabulary by comparing things. "Look at this! Even though Grandpa is taller than Grandma, there are only three apples and two oranges in the fruit bowl." Movement and play are excellent ways to discover new things. Parents should be aware that their children are learning while they play.

Discuss the Stories you've Read

Even with babies, it's never too early to begin reading aloud to your child. Hearing words expands vocabulary and aids in developing neural pathways in the brain. There is a lot of emphasis on the basics when discussing stories, but many parents don't see it when reading aloud.

Positive Parenting Strategies

Prosaically results for both parents and children can be linked to excellent parenting practices, according to research. Consequently, practitioners have devised and executed a variety of programs to encourage positive parenting.

Home visiting improves the quality of the mother-infant bond by raising their level of parental sensitivity. Psychiatrists go to the homes of high-risk mothers in to teach them how to better respond to their children's cues, which will strengthen the bond between the youngster and their parents. Every week, a family educator teaches how to foster healthy parent-child relationships and participate in their children's daily activities. This program teaches nonviolent discipline, anger management, social problem-solving, and other approaches designed to shield children from aggression and violence. Families experiencing divorce or separation can benefit from an empirically-supported program. Divorce-affected families can better care for their children when the parents know how to raise, discipline, and keep them safe. The primary purpose of the New Beginnings Programs to help children cope with the stress of this tough period.

When a child dies, a grieving family can benefit from a program called the Family Bereavement Program. The goal of an intervention is to help parents and children cope with the loss of a parent. Many resilience-enhancing parenting skills (e.g., active listening, effective rules, helping children's coping and establishing family relationships) were learned in a supportive group environment for bereaved parents.

The Positive Parent is a guide for parents who want to raise happy children. Aiming to improve positive parenting by educating parents about child development and alternative methods of raising children, this online course also aimed to connect parents for mutual support to help them feel more confident in their parenting abilities and content with the way their children are being raised.

Healthy Families Alaska Programs: the goal of this home visiting program was to help Alaskan parents be better parents with better outcomes for their children's development. Parents and their children benefited from the work of paraprofessionals who promoted better attitudes toward parenting, better interactions between parents and children, better knowledge of child development, and a better home environment.

The Strengthening Families Program: this primary prevention curriculum has been widely utilized to educate a wide range of good parenting skills to parents and guardians. Parenting skills such as positive interactions with children, positive communication, effective discipline, rewarding positive behavior, and the use of family meetings to promote organization have been taught in the programmed following family systems and cognitive-behavioral philosophies. The overall purpose was to improve children's social and life skills, as well as boost the protective factors of children and their families.

Emotional problems and aggression in children can be reduced through a group-based intervention that has been widely implemented and evaluated. There were 12-20 weekly group meetings for parent groups; the topics ranged from relationship building and positive discipline to helping children get ready for school and improve their academic performance. This program worked well for kids with ADHD.

Multiple evaluation studies of positive parenting programs administered across Spain are featured in a special issue of Psychosocial Intervention. Programs given in groups, at home, and online are all featured, with all geared toward providing positive parenting support services. Understanding which parents benefit most from evidence-based programs promoting positive parenting among parents and visiting family support services can be found in the Journal of Family Issues.

The Triple P Program provides parents of high-risk children with the knowledge, confidence, and skills they need to enhance their children's psychological health and well-being. Although varied, one of the primary goals is to help youngsters learn how to better control their emotions.

Positive Parenting Style

According to positive parenting research, a loving, but firm parenting style is associated with a beneficial adolescent outcomes, including academic achievement and social development. An authoritative parenting style is defined as an approach that includes a good balance of parenting qualities: assertive but not intrusive, demanding but responsive, supportive in terms of discipline while not being punitive, and supportive in terms of discipline while not being punitive. As well as having an authoritative parenting style, it is considered a developing parenting style may help children achieve beneficial results.

Affection (i.e., through positive expressions of warmth toward the child), responsiveness (i.e., by paying attention to a child's cues), encouragement (i.e., by supporting a child's abilities and interests), and teaching (i.e., by incorporating play and conversation to support a child's cognitive development) are all characteristics of developmental parenting. Developmental parenting and authoritative parenting have a number of characteristics in common, and both are considered desirable parenting styles.

Taken together, positive parenting practices that work for raising healthy, happy children reveal that positive parenting styles enhance a child's autonomy. Here's how:

Providing opportunities for inquiry and participation in decision-making

Paying close attention to and reacting to the needs of a kid

Making use of efficient communication techniques

Paying attention to and exercising control over a child's emotional expression

Positive conduct should be rewarded and encouraged

Establishing clear standards and expectations is essential

Making consistent punishments and rewards for appropriate conduct

Making sure there is enough supervision and monitoring

Being good role model

Making healthy family experiences a priority is an important step

Briefly said, positive parents encourage children's healthy development and inner spirit by being caring, supporting, firm and consistent while also being engaged. Such parents go above and beyond just articulating their expectations; they demonstrate their commitment to their children by serving as excellent role models.

Teach them How to Reframe their Thinking

Resilience is defined as the capacity to reinterpret obstacles in a manner that makes them seem less intimidating. Reframing is an extremely useful talent. The ability to concentrate on what they have rather than what they have lost can be beneficial through times of stress or disappointment. In order to develop this talent, accept their displeasure and gently guide them away from focusing on what the situation has cost them and toward the possibilities the problem may have provided.

Fearing the Unknown – But with Help

Being able to face fear is very powerful (within the boundaries of self-preservation, of course, remaining alive is also empowering), but to do so, they need the appropriate support – just as we all do – from others. When it comes to things, kids may be quite black and white, so when presented with a challenging situation, the options might seem limited to two. Tackle it straight on or avoid it at all costs. A third alternative, though, is to take little steps toward it while feeling encouraged and in control.

Make no Hasty Attempts to Save them

Kids learn how to find their feet in the little window of time between falling and getting back up again. Of course, there are instances when picking them up and placing them in a stable environment is precisely what they need to find the fortitude to continue ahead. The most important thing is to avoid doing it on a regular basis. Exposure to stresses and difficulties they can handle throughout childhood will guarantee that they are better prepared to cope with stress when they reach the adult stage of life. There is growing evidence that early experiences cause favorable changes in the prefrontal cortex (the part of the brain that tells you "cool down, you've got this"), which will buffer against the harmful consequences of future stress. Consider it similar to immunization: a little amount of the pathogen, whether a virus or anything stressful, aids in the development of resistance or the protection against the more severe for.

Meet them Where they are

It is not about never falling down to be resilient. It's all about getting back on your feet again. We have all experienced emotional anguish, setbacks, loss, and despair at some point in our lives. Despite the fact that feelings might be a bit intrusive at times, they always have a valid cause. The goal for children is to learn to appreciate their sentiments (especially when negative), but not to allow them to take control and drive them to danger. For example, feelings of sadness or loss may cause us to wish to retreat for a short period of time. It is during the withdrawal phase that information is considered, digested, and processed to restore equilibrium. If this process is hastened, even if done in the name of resilience, it will remain as a quiet rumble and manifest via behavior, sometimes at radically unexpected moments.

Inform them that you have Confidence in their Ability to Deal

When someone is afraid of failing, it isn't so much about the loss as it is about the concern that they (or you) will not be able to deal it. What you believe counts a great deal: it truly does. You're the one they'll seek for feedback on how things are going. If you trust in their ability to deal with the setbacks that will inevitably occur, they will believe in themselves as well. This is not always a simple task. We frequently feel every bump, bruise, tumble, and failure that comes our way. It's okay, no matter how long it takes. Kids will make a decision based on what you decide.

Make Time for your own Imagination and Play

Problem-solving is a creative process that requires imagination. Anything that helps them improve their problem-solving abilities will help them become more resilient. Children are inherently curious, inquisitive, and imaginative beings. Give them room and time to play and be creative, and the rest will be taken care of.

Allow them to Express themselves

Try to refrain from taking on their issues. (I know it's tempting, but it's true!) Instead, act as a sounding board while they navigate their way. Their thoughts are being processed and strengthened. A light bright enough to read by might be produced by the sparks shooting through the atmosphere. While you should guide them, also allow them to communicate and come up with their own ideas wherever possible. You provide the safest environment possible in which to explore and try new things. Solving problems is a great skill, and the time they spend talking with you and coming up with ideas allows them to develop them to the fullest. Allow them the freedom to explore and roam about in their tremendous potential.

Optimism should be Encouraged

Optimism has been identified as one of the most important traits of the resilient. Because of one's experiences, the brain may be rewired to become more hopeful in the future. Give your tiny person the perspective that the glass is only half empty to see the situation differently. This does not imply that their feelings are invalid. Make a point of acknowledging their point of view on the world and then introduce them to another.

Create Sentiments of Competence and a Sense of Mastery in your Students

Create an environment where children can feel good about themselves, and they will be more likely to perform difficult tasks. Your actions will demonstrate your support every time you recognize their strengths, the courageous things they accomplish, and their effort facing a challenging task. Every time you encourage them to make independent choices, they start to feel in control, reducing tendency to react negatively to future stress. It makes it easier to cope with obstacles in the future.

Building Self-Confidence

Parents should know that there are several things they can do to help their children develop confidence. They are to provide a loving environment, be highly involved (and patient!), and impart lots of encouragement when a new skill is learned or a particular effort is made. Positive reinforcement is the way parents can help their children develop confidence, character, and resilience. However, understanding why self-confidence is such a critical contributor to good cognitive and emotional growth and long-term success is vital.

Children with self-confidence have faith in their qualities and capabilities. As a result, these4 youngsters are more inclined to push themselves in a learning setting. Self-assured children have faith in their abilities to control their behavior, gain new skills, and overcome challenges as they grow. According to research, they're also more likely to get along with others and demonstrate a more favorable reaction to social situations in which sharing and taking turns are involved.

However, self-confidence does not happen by chance. Babies are not born with a strong sense of self or knowledge that they are separate entities from their parents. Children's self-confidence, character, and resilience -- all essential features for personal development and intricately tied to one another -- are shaped in large part by their interactions and experiences with the people in their environment.

In most cases, parents are the first instructors of their children. Children learn how to cope with the world around them by observing and experiencing it in their home environment. To help their children become self-confident, parents can use various methods to set them up for academic and social success.

Establishing rituals with your newborn or toddler can help you both feel more secure.

Routines assist a youngster in feeling comfortable and secure by providing a sense of control. Whether it's a nighttime routine that includes changing into pajamas, brushing teeth, and reading a tale, or an afternoon nap after lunch, clean-up, and a puzzle activity, routines are essential. An organized, regular day will help your kid navigate and explore his environment without being concerned about what is going on. Furthermore, according to specialists, children who follow a pattern better cope with stressful or unexpected events.

Set a good example by being yourself.

Children will learn to have a confident mentality from their parents. Thus, it is crucial to be a positive role model by maintaining control over your emotions, moderating your responses to situations, remaining persistent in the face of obstacles, and verbally demonstrating how you cope with strong emotions or complex challenges. Remaining optimistic and engaging in positive self-talk are all examples.

Create chances for children to play and to learn.

Playing, exploring, discovering interests, overcoming challenges, solving problems, and overcoming challenges are important ways to help your child build self-confidence. You'll be laying a solid foundation for your child's future success.

Develop self-help abilities in children from a young age.

Confidence is connected with competence, so give your kid duties (such as tidying up toys or helping with pet feeding) and empower them to solve issues for themselves. You will be setting them up for a successful introduction to school. They will feel more confident as they become helpful, important, successful, and valuable.

Chapter 30
10 Ways to Foster Self-esteem and Help a Child Develop a Growth Mindset

According to Dweck's and other neuroscientific studies, the brain behaves similarly to a muscle that becomes stronger with training. When we repeat the same knowledge to our children over and over again, we see a shift in their attitudes and ability to learn. Being able to help young people in realizing that the problems we experience while learning new and challenging things is normal is a sign that the brain's neural connections are forming. A such it becomes a highly powerful tool for altering their mentality. Motivational boosts, a willingness to take on new activities, and more positive reactions to failure are just a few of the benefits that children and adolescents experience when they understand how the brains work and to use it. It may be beneficial for a child who has been encountering difficulty in a particular area of their learning to adopt a development attitude.

Through our assistance in establishing this mentality, we provide them with the understanding that if they put up the necessary effort, they will almost certainly see change. When children and adolescents realize that their intelligence and skill levels are not innate but can be developed and improved, they become naturally engaged and organically motivated to problem-solve and acquire new knowledge and skills by putting in the required time and effort.

As a result, it is our obligation as parents to encourage our children's intrinsic curiosity about the world around them while simultaneously enabling them to make mistakes and learn from them via practice, repetition, and trial and error, among other methods. We improve on the possibility that our child will acquire a lifelong enthusiasm for learning and education as a result of these efforts.

In order for children to get smarter, they must first cultivate a development attitude, which teaches them that there is actually no such thing as a "fixed intelligence." One of the most significant benefits of instilling a development attitude in children is that they are more likely to succeed in school. Why? If youngsters learn they can increase their intellect by simply working hard, in the same way that a muscle develops with repeated usage, they will come to realize that the only constraints to their talents are those they impose upon themselves.

We must educate our children that the most important component of any assignment is the effort and practice put in since it is only in this way that they will achieve their goals. Instead of focusing on how well they performed, young people could begin to think about how they might improve the performance. Furthermore, by refraining from exaggerating our child's accomplishments and their consequences, and instead emphasizing the effort put forth, we are supporting our children in comprehending the intrinsic significance of just "taking part." Thus, children are urged to adopt an attitude of "effort over outcome", which indicates that the process of doing new activities becomes fulfilling in and of itself, with it being the ultimate goal.

Assist Them in Discovering Their Uniqueness: Make a List

Self-esteem is derived from a positive self-image and knowledge of one's own abilities, as well as what distinguishes oneself from other people. To achieve long-lasting improvement in your child's confidence and behavior, the most effective method is for them to become more internally motivated. You, as a parent, are really important in this process. You are helping him or her now so that he or she will not need your help or anyone else's in the future as the child will be prepared for the difficulties of life.

First of all, help them find their own unique abilities. In order for your kids to discover activities they like and "naturally" have a better facility for, when they are young and inexperienced, make them explore a variety of different things. The process of learning and developing will become more enjoyable as a result, and they will be less inclined to quit when things get hard. They will be enjoying themselves by just learning and taking part . It is crucial that you as a parent praise your kid not for achievements but for the effort put in. You could say something like "It was so good seeing you do all of the activities you have done today and learn how to be better every time! I'm so proud of you for this" instead of "I'm so proud that you won, you're the best."

The next step is assisting them in creating a list of their abilities and "gifts", such as being excellent at a sport (football, gymnastics, dance, etc.) or a musical instrument, or at reading, drawing, and singing. Remember that you should not expect your kid to be super great, especially if they have never tried the activity before. Include an activity on their list if they are decent at it, don't struggle, and they enjoy learning it. This list can be extended to include being a "helper," a "career," and similar abstract characteristics. Make certain you showcase their abilities in a manner that does not come off as evaluative praise or draws attention to their inherent nature. The goal is to instill confidence in youngsters and convince them that they have the ability to develop those qualities and traits that distinguish them from others.

Find Something That Will Challenge Them to Help Them Develop Perseverance

Confidence may also be gained by effort and triumph over adversity. It's critical that your children not limit themselves to simply doing things that come naturally and seek out (age-appropriate) difficulties they can conquer to grow. Providing children with the opportunity to discover their own answers to difficulties has been shown to boost confidence, allowing them to realize they are capable of overcoming obstacles without assistance or praise. It is critical to allow your kid to struggle when confronted with adversity to provide them with the chance to develop tenacity, persistence, and grit.

If they are not facing any difficulty at the moment, you might consider letting your kids try something new and challenging. Being in a constant comfort zone can be dangerous, as boredom can push older kids into feeling new emotions in an unhealthy way such as through alcohol, drugs, or violence.

If they are already having difficulty, rather than "saving them" by meddling, you may assist them by proposing different techniques to do what they are attempting. Remember to tell them that they are still learning, are at the beginning of the process and the beginning of life and that they have so much time to discover new things and be good at them.

It is important to say to your kids, especially when they exhibit dissatisfaction during a difficulty something along the lines, of "I'm not good at this." You may also answer "you're not good at this YET." When used in conjunction with the word "yet", it serves to rise to the pinnacle of a development mentality rather than a fixed attitude, since it informs youngsters that this is a transitory situation and they may make improvement with effort.

Celebrate Both Successes and Failures

Children must believe that it is normal and essential to face obstacles and make errors in order to develop a growth mindset and to be resilient as they grow. Eventually, they will be able to learn from them. Helping them realize that failure may be seen as a 'first attempt in learning" and that taking action and failing should result in less regret than not trying in the first place.

When your kid encounters difficulties, begin by expressing empathy for their trouble or emotion (for example, "You appear to actually have had a lot of difficulty with your math assignment; arithmetic may be challenging at times"). Do not underestimate what they are feeling. Parents tend to say something like "This is not that serious. You are overreacting; don't be dramatic, life is harder, you're just starting. I do understand why you may think that life is really hard and becomes harder as you get older." Parents have to deal with the world of work, financial and health problems, and so many other difficult things, but your kid doesn't. He or she will discover how hard life is later, but for now in his or her little world, the problem they are facing is enormous. They are not overreacting; they are kids - inexperienced sweet creatures. This is true when they grow up and become adolescents. By underestimating their problems you might:

Make them feel weak or incapable of facing problems.

Discourage them to talk to you when they have a problem and that could be dangerous as they get older.

Make them feel alone or angry.

Expressing empathy will let them open up with you, express their feelings and create a moment in which they feel allowed to be weak and rest under your loving arms. Assist them in developing ways to make things less difficult, such as through "chunking" the process of breaking down larger difficulties into smaller ones to make them more manageable and feasible.

In situations where you believe there is room for improvement, rather than directly giving them "constructive criticism", try asking, "Are you happy with the result?" (This allows your child to tell you what they would like to improve.) "Do you think it is possible for you to do better next time?" The chance for self-evaluation allows them to feel more empowered and accountable for the solutions that they choose in an effort to make things better for everyone.

Descriptive Praise and a Description of the "Process"

Instead of focusing on the outcome, consider your child's approach and the learning process. When you praise your kid for each step they take, he or she is more likely to comprehend that each is necessary to reach the desired outcome. Instead of just saying, "Wow, this is really fantastic!" offer your child a question such as, "How did you actually do this part?" or describe what you have seen or what you think is remarkable such as, "Wow, your chicken painting looks very realistic!"

In response to your exhibiting an interest in their work and the process by which it was produced, your child will be more likely to recognize and analyze his or her own successes (like you did) and be more inclined to share them with you even when they get older.

After a great success, you may remember the process the child to the point where they are. You could bring up memories of when they first started that specific activity, the difficulties and the learning process - that is way more important that the success. This method of describing what they already achieved can be useful if they are facing a difficulty or if they have failed at something because you are focusing your attention on the process. Your kid should become proud of themself or at least proud of their effort.

You want them to think, "Yes, I worked really hard to get this achievement; it will be worthwhile to put in the same amount of effort again in the future." Encouraging children to adopt this mindset helps them become less fearful of making errors as they begin to see that they are a necessary part of the learning process and not to be avoided at all cost.

Rather Than Praising Their General Behavior, Praise Particular Behaviors

Kids need to feel special, especially when growing and building their confidence. They see on TV that superheroes, princesses, fairies etc. have in common is a superpower, something that makes them unique and strong. Children are often inspired by them, want to be like them - or pretend to. But for the fragile kid, seeing all of those special beings can be overwhelming. He or she might wonder "what makes me special?" If he or she is not confident and has no self-esteem, they could think they are not special and are useless since they have nothing that makes them different from others.

You as a parent should know why your offspring is special, and you have to be specific about it. If you praise their general behavior or say something like "You're the best kid in the world," they will not believe you and their problem won't be solved. Instead, take your time to think about his or her spirit in order and praise it.

You can say, "You are usually very kind and helpful. I enjoyed your assistance in helping Granny get into and out of her chair when she was here. It was something very good and kind to do, that is impressive."

"Staged" eavesdropping, such as praising your kid in front of a spouse or another, may also be an excellent approach to recognize one of your child's unique acts and make them feel special. Remember that this trick doesn't always work so, think about the possible reaction of your kid. Some children are shy and even if they like praise, getting it in front of others could make them feel embarrassed, especially if they are older.

Be Careful with Your Praise

If your kid completes a task they are meant to complete, refrain from congratulating them. If you lavish praise on your child's every accomplishment, he or she will either disregard what you are saying or grow reliant on it for self-affirmation. In the case of carrying something to the table or throwing their clothes into the laundry, a simple "thank you" is an adequate expression of gratitude.

Having said that, some parents have a propensity to "under praise" their children out of worry that doing the reverse will "spoil" their child's development. Understand that this is also harmful, since your children want encouragement and positive reinforcement from you to feel good about themselves and their actions. We all agree that life will not spoil our children but our praises can make them strong enough to face the difficulties of life without losing themselves.

Just because it was hard for us and our parents didn't put in so much time, affection, or effort in our education doesn't mean that we should put our children under the same pressure. Times have changed and everything is more complex, even for youngsters and in ways we might not fully understand. We should do our best to assist them during the building process.

I was afraid of my dad when I was a little girl; today what children (and adolescents even more) have to deal with is scary and as parents, we should not be part of the problem but a safe refuge where they can rest, talk, and learn how to be strong in the storm.

Make it Personal

Remember that what you want is for your children to be able to evaluate themselves and become more self-aware of their own actions. Children who lack a healthy sense of self-awareness may develop into "praise addicts", who grow reliant on you to tell them whether or not they are doing a good job. We have the job of preparing our children to face situations in which we are not present and cannot emotionally or physically help them. In order to do so we should be careful and notice if our hard work is going in this direction or not. It is easier than you think: a good way is asking questions. By asking questions, you make your kids think and evaluate themselves.

For example, instead of saying, "I'm very proud of you," consider asking your kid, "You have worked hard and done well on this exam, are you proud of yourself?" or "Are you satisfied with the result?" to assist them in developing their capacity to assess themselves and recognize their accomplishments. And if they respond affirmatively, you may easily follow up with, "I am proud of you as well."!".

Tell Them Inspirational Stories

Children are not all the same; some of them find it hard to speak or they hate when someone talks about them or their life. This is something you must accept, respect and remember that it is not a big deal. Even if they will not listen to you when talking about "their things" (this is true especially for adolescents), they will listen to stories about someone else. Now is your time to become a storyteller and find a story that contain some useful advice for your kid.

For example, if he or she is struggling with a sport, you can tell them the story of someone you know who was having difficulties but in the end achieved what she or he wanted. You can also search for stories on the internet. It Is better if you don't make up those stories, especially if the kid knows you are lying. Moreover, if you give them a name, they can search the history of this person, learn more about their life and how they achieved what they wanted. As such, they become a hero for your kid. Remember that it is not necessary that these examples are real life persons; they could also be superheroes or characters of a book. Be creative!

Emphasize the Good and Minimize the Bad

Studies have shown that for youngsters to be driven and confident, they need at least three times the number of positive remarks as negative ones. Children with low self-esteem and adolescents tend to be negative about themselves, and you should not add more weight on their shoulders. Of course, it is normal that you as a parent have to correct your child's behavior, but please do it in a constructive way and afterward, remember that your child is still a good person by making positive remarks. Maybe for you it's obvious that a single mistake doesn't make your kid a bad guy, but children with low self-esteem might easily think, "I'm a disaster and everyone thinks that."

"I see that you've done it this way, but I think that you can do better. For example, think about making it in this way...." rather than "No, that's not the way to do this" might be used in a situation where your kid could have done something better or didn't know how to solve a problem and made a mistake. By doing so, you will teach your kid that mistakes are an occasion to do better and not being with themselves. They will peacefully think about how to do better next time rather than focusing on what happened now. Nobody can change the past, but you can learn from it and change the future. Showing how your kid can do better will instill in him or her a sense of optimism in their outlook on life by presenting the glass half-full viewpoint rather than the glass half-empty. Every time your kids makes a mistake (because as humans, wat always make mistakes), they will not be focused on the mess made but how they can do better next time.

Exhibit the Leadership Through Example

Children often copy their parents and their thinking, therefore for your children to acquire a growth mindset, the home should ideally sett the appropriate example. Your job is to model a development mindset for your children as much as possible and be aware of when you are not setting the ideal example for your children.

If you have a propensity to use negative words, such as "I'm not very good at this" or "This is really tough," attempt to replace them with remarks that encourage growth and development. Using the examples above, you might say, "I'm not quite as good as I'd want to be at this, I need to put in more work" or "I haven't quite mastered this, it will actually really take a lot of effort, but I know it will be worth it in the end." Avoid using phrases like "I absolutely screwed this up" when something doesn't turn out the way you wanted it to. Instead, use phrases like , "Although I didn't get it perfect this time, I learned a lot from the process and I can't wait to give it another go." Take advantage of as many chances as possible to showcase a positive attitude and demonstrate to your children that you will always endeavor to maintain a glass half full viewpoint, especially during difficult circumstances.

When you have a positive attitude, you are proving to your children that there are benefits to be gained from every error or difficulty. You're not only helping your kid but also yourself. It's never too late to actually learn how to love ourselves a little bit more or how to deal with life in a more positive way.

Chapter 31
The 25 Most Effective Self-Esteem Activities You Can Do Right Now

Is your youngster proud of their accomplishments, or do they tend to be too critical of themselves? With the help of this exercise, you may learn more about the question.

Chart or drawing paper, magazine cutouts of adjectives, glue, color pen or sketch pen, and other materials

How to do it:

Instruct your children to write down a list of terms that define them on a sheet of paper. It might have actually a bad or good connotation.

Then instruct them to concentrate only on the positive things others have said about them and compile a list of these.

Place the child's picture in the middle of the drawing or chart page (optional)

To get started, have the youngster fill in the blanks surrounding the image with positive phrases and adjectives that she can identify with.

Place the drawing sheet of paper in her room as a means of reinforcing her positive self-image and ideas.

Make a list of all your accomplishments.

Reminding the youngster of their accomplishments is a great technique to increase their self-esteem.

How to do it:

Give your child a pen and paper or a notebook if they are old enough.

Begin by jotting down a list of your life's accomplishments on the front page, allowing room at the bottom for further entries later.

You may also ask the kid to make a list of her accomplishments every day before she goes to bed, which will serve as a reminder of her potential.

Insist on the fact that failures are not only acceptable but also necessary. When your kid successfully navigates a challenging situation, take time to acknowledge their accomplishment.

I am terrified, however

Children often experience fear. Here is an exercise for youngsters to participate in which they may confront their concerns and speak about them.

How to do it:

Instruct your kid to make a list of all the things she is frightened of doing. Her fear of going to swimming lessons, for example, might be justified. Alternatively, she may be afraid of giving a class presentation.

The second stage is for them to visualize themselves performing what they are afraid of. Consider the possibility of joining that swim team or conversing with that individual.

Every time the youngster puts down anything they are frightened of, ask them to write down what might happen if they did it. Along with the unfavorable consequence, ask them to write something about potential good outcomes to go with it.

For Younger Children

The Dancing Chain Game

This game is actually a great way for little ones to develop their social skills while having fun with friends or family at the same time. It involves dancing or moving the body, which little boys and girls often find extremely fun. To play this game, the first person begins by doing a short dance move or a movement such as a jump or a twirl. The next person has to copy the first person's movement and then do one of their own. This chain continues, and each person completes all the dance moves that their friends or family members did before adding on a dance move of their own.

This game is important for younger children to develop their social skills because not only are they participating in a group activity, but they must also pay attention to everyone else around them and dance for others to see. The children will not even know that this game is educational because they will be having so much fun with it.

Three-Legged Race or Wheelbarrow Race

Having a good old-fashioned three-legged or a wheelbarrow race are two great ways to help kids develop their social skills and teamwork skills. These games are fun to play with multiple siblings, at a birthday party, or with cousins at a family get-together. It can be played with smaller groups too!

To begin, two kids will stand two of their ankles next to each other. A parent will then tie their ankles together using a piece of ribbon or a necktie or something else similar. Then, the kids will hold onto each other and run as fast as they can from the starting line to the finish line, ensuring that they synchronize their steps to avoid toppling over one another. If you have many people, you can have one big race, which will be fun for all ages.

A wheelbarrow race is similar, but it begins with one child lying face-down on the floor, his/her hands pressed to the ground on either side of his/her chest. The second child will lift the first child's legs off the ground and hold onto his/her ankles, while the first child will hold the rest of his/her own body up by his/her arms. He/she will use his/her arms to walk along the floor or the grass, and the other child will try to walk as if he/she is pushing a wheelbarrow to the finish line!

These two games are great for developing social skills because they both require immense teamwork to take even a single step. This will get each pair of partners working together toward a common goal, which is important for developing social skills. This also requires communication skills, important in both teamwork and social skill development in general.

For Older Children

When children get a bit older, things change and it can be difficult for you as a parent to find things for your child to do that do not involve a computer, game system, or an organized sport. Children become pickier as they age, and it is not easy to occupy them anymore, especially not with games and activities that they know are educational.

Playing Chess

While this game only involves two players, it can be a great game for teaching your child to develop analytical skills and social skills since he/she needs to conduct himself/herself maturely and patiently to sit through a full game of chess. Teaching your child how to play a game like chess will be an experience and a skill he/she will remember for the rest of his/her life. He/she will probably even teach his/her child how to play chess. Chess is a great game that has been around for centuries, and now that your child is old enough to learn, this can be a great activity to share that is both educational and amusing.

Playing Scrabble

Scrabble is another game that your child can learn and play once he/she has reached an age where he/she is old enough to understand and remember the rules, as there are many in a game like this. This game is great for children between the ages of nine and twelve, and it will help them develop their language skills and learn a deeper vocabulary. This game will also help them to learn social skills, as this game usually involves up to 4 players and will require both individual and team work.

Limbo

Limbo is a fun game to play with children who are rapidly growing taller and taller as the months pass, and the game will be different for them each time they play. As their height changes, the game of Limbo will change for them, and this can be fun to watch as a parent. You can use anything as your pole for limbo, from the long branch of a tree to a meter-long ruler stick to a piece of string!

This game can be played with other family members, or your child can play this with his/her friends. If you play as well, your child will surely have a laugh watching you try to slide your body underneath the Limbo. Limbo will teach social skills as it involves many moving parts, meaning that all the people playing must work together. There will be people in charge of holding the Limbo stick, people taking their turn trying to walk under, and people watching to ensure that nobody touches the Limbo pole. These people must communicate and work together, leading to the development of stronger social skills.

Drawing Portraits

Drawing portraits is a fun and relaxing way for your child to spend time with you or his/her friends or siblings inside the house. This is a fun rainy-day activity that will keep your children occupied and teach them valuable social skills. Each person will have a piece of paper and a pencil. Each person will draw someone else sitting with them. If there are two people, they will draw each other. They will sit across the table from one another and draw portraits of each other simultaneously. When they have finished, they can then compare their portraits with one another and even exchange them. This is a great activity for teaching social skills as it challenges your child to pay close attention to another person—so close that he/she needs to draw his/her face. This is a good way to show your child that paying attention to others is important and can result in something beautiful!

Chapter 32
A Self-esteem-Building Activity Between a Mother and her Daughter

Mother-daughter interactions tend to be both solid and riddled with conflict. This exercise uses the mother-daughter relationship to help a girl improve her self-esteem.

How to do it:

Using stencils, create two posters with 'ME' stenciled on them. This will allow you to fill in the blanks with content later.

Create two more posters, one with the words "MY MOM" stenciled on it and the other with the phrases "MY GIRL" written on them.

Make two "ME" posters for the kid, as well as an "MY MOM" poster, and encourage her to fill in the blanks with good things about herself and her mother. Leave the remaining two to the care of your mother.

Provide an opportunity for them to trade posters or read aloud the praises they have for one another.

Performing a task with a purpose

When people realize that someone has faith in them, their confidence is immediately boosted. What better way to demonstrate to your kid that you believe in them than to delegate responsibility for a household chore?

How to do it:

Please make a list of activities your kid can do to help the environment and the creatures in their immediate vicinity. Among household chores are walking the dog, watering the plants, and sweeping the floor.

Every time the youngster completes the work successfully, give them a sincere compliment but do not go overboard.

If they make a mistake, assist them in correcting the error, but do not focus on the error. Chores may help your youngster develop self-confidence by giving them something to do.

Visualization

Our negative ideas can become so overwhelming that we cannot envisage anything positive. This activity can be beneficial if your child is going through a similar phase.

How to do it:

Investigate why your kid believes they are unworthy or what they are frightened of doing.

For example, if they are concerned about school or their sports success, they should concentrate on those concerns.

In any instance, ask them to visualize and write down what they believe would be the perfect situation.

Afterwards, instruct your youngster to shut their eyes and visualize the perfect situation, as well as how she would feel if it were true.

During this exercise, have students write down their feelings as they pictured the perfect circumstance and what they thought about themselves.

Changing one's inner monologue

When you have poor self-confidence, you will engage in negative self-talk. It may be beneficial to point out inappropriate language and encourage your youngster to avoid speaking critically about themselves. Using this technique, you may transform negative discussions with yourself into more positive ones.

How to do it:

Two columns should be drawn on a piece of paper. Excellent or positive self-talk should be written on one side of the article, while bad or negative self-talk should be reported.

Instruct your youngster to create a list of all negative comments about themselves and place them in the Bad self-talk section.

After that, ask your youngster to change the negative phrases into positive ones to complete the sentence. Declarative remarks should be concise and tailored to your child's particular qualities or abilities.

You might assist the youngster by setting an example for them from the outset. You may describe how you transform your negative self-talk into a positive one and how this has benefited you.

More helpful than having children read a book or attend a lecture on positive self-worth is getting youngsters involved in activities that remind them of their skills and self-worth. Please use your power to make them feel good about their appearance. Recognize that the most effective strategy for developing a healthy sense of self is to work through the inevitable blunders and disconnections.

Chapter 33
Other Activities that will Help Develop Confidence and Self-Esteem

Developing self-awareness and goals:

Setting goals is also a great way to achieve something over a long period of time, as it helps to develop self-esteem and allows children to make mistakes that will teach valuable lessons.

Here are some ideas that can help develop their self-awareness:

Ask your child (ideally in a family meeting) to share what they consider to be their greatest strength and their greatest achievement to date. Does their self-evaluation match your own opinion?

Ask them to share one or two goals/dreams they'd like to achieve in the next 12 months. Ask them to be specific about the nature of this goal and how they will achieve it. For example, if they want to be able to play the piano in front of an audience in 12 months, or if they'd like to be part of the school's football team, what are the steps to achieving this. If they come up with negative self-talk, find ways to show them why this is a 'fixed mindset' and how a growth mindset can help them to achieve their goal(s).

Teaching them how their brain works:

This a great way of demonstrating to them that when we practice something new, the "neural connections" that our synapses make get stronger and the easier things get. Here are actually some useful books that can help you initiate a discussion with your child about how their brain works:

For younger children: Your Fantastic Elastic Brain Stretch it, Shape it by JoAnn Deak.

For older children: My First Book About the Brain by Patricia J. Wynne

Improving memory:

As Dominic O'Brien's story demonstrates, a good memory can be a great confidence booster. You can help your children develop their memory from an early age by playing memory games with them.

Here are a couple of games that will help improve their memory:

You have most probably already heard of the game: "I went to the market and bought?" This is a great way to develop memory because creating a story around a situation is a proven method to help people remember things. One person starts by saying, "I went to the market and bought" and chooses an item. Each participant takes a turn and must recite what the others have said in the right order whilst also adding an extra item to the list.

Another enjoyable and useful game is to place 10 items on a table and ask your child to memorize the objects for a minute or two. Then ask them to turn their back, allowing you to remove an item. They then look at the remaining objects and have a limited time (depending on their age) to guess which one you removed.

Teaching them about how to use their body to increase their confidence:

Body language can influence confidence. If you can teach your children to show confidence through their body language, this will affect their state of mind and they will feel more confident as a result, which becomes a self-reinforcing cycle.

Breathing is also a great way to increase confidence by reducing stress and anxiety in challenging situations. Deep, mindful breathing - which means breathing from the belly - is one of the most effective ways of reducing stress, allowing us to make calm and rational decisions. Breathing for around three minutes per day from an early age (and increasing this as they grow) is important to practice with children as it helps give them a sense of control over their own emotions and reactions to things.

Arts and Crafts

Arts and crafts are a wonderful outlet for everyone who wants to express themselves. Organize a poster-making session with your children to celebrate them. You may supply your kid with a variety of periodicals, newspapers, and images, and then let them make a collage depicting how they perceive themselves. Pottery is really extremely relaxing, and it enables youngsters to express themselves creatively. It is possible to get a range of air-dry clays in a variety of colors at your local arts and crafts shop. For example, you might take your kid to a craft shop and let them choose a project that they would want to do - art is fantastic since it enables one to be creative while also providing immediate pleasure.

Another excellent tip for fostering confidence in children is to assist them in compiling a list of everything that makes them joyful. This may seem to be a goofy tool, but it is really rather useful. Focusing on positive circumstances and objects can open your child's eyes to the many different ways they may keep themselves happy!

Positive Trait Game

Your child's self-esteem will be boosted as a result of participating in the "Positive Trait Game", which will be good to expand his or her vocabulary. With the use of a word, players must describe a Positive Trait that they can observe in the other player. The important thing to remember about the game is that it is all about coming up with a term that starts with a certain letter of the alphabet that the other participants choose! This enables your kid to have a good attitude about oneself, as well as to notice and appreciate their own unique characteristics and abilities. They will grow up with an understanding of their own personal strengths.

Involve your kid in a range of activities that will help them discover and develop their own unique talents and skills. Be open-minded and enroll them in summer sessions, which may include activities that are unfamiliar to them in order to extend their horizons and improve their abilities. Whatever happens, even if they do not have a good time, they will have gained valuable experience.

Stand in front of the Mirror

Allow your youngster to stand in front of a mirror and say something kind about himself or herself. Confidence can be built by looking in the mirror and saying things like "I'm a great person, I'm smart and confident, and I'm going to do the best I can at everything today." Over time, seeing yourself say things like "I'm a great person, I'm smart and confident, and I'm going to do the best I can at everything today" has an impact.

Of course, sports, particularly martial arts, may help youngsters gain confidence and improve their self-esteem tremendously. In my opinion, the courses provided are among the finest available on the market right now. Providing your kid with intellectual challenges via activities such as puzzles and brain teasers may also assist to build confidence. Whatever stimulates the other side of the brain in the long run helps youngsters develop stronger thinking and planning abilities in the long run is beneficial.

The confidence that comes from inside a kid when confronted with a variety of challenges and circumstances in the real world will be enhanced if they have an open mind and are able to "think outside of the box." Some activities may seem to be fairly infantile, yet they have the potential to create a lasting effect on young children. Those impressions will linger with them for the rest of their life. Have you taken a moment to examine yourself in the mirror recently? Do you enjoy what you've seen so far? Little actions and encouraging words may have a significant impact on how someone views their own self-worth and appearance.

Feel Good! Feel Bad!

Have your youngster participate in our "Feel Good! Feel Bad!" game. Inquire as to if they can recall a moment when they were depressed or sick. Display how to walk with their shoulders stooped, heads down, and feet shuffling about in a circular motion. Then ask them to recall a period that was both thrilling and joyful for them. Ask them to recall a memorable occasion and then instruct them to jump up and down and move about the room with their heads up and their shoulders back. When your youngster has grasped the concept, declare the start of the game! Offer them a "win" prize at the conclusion of the game, such as a cupcake or something, then play the game with them for a few minutes after that. "Feel bad!" you may say to them as you droop about with them. Then exclaim, "Feel Good!" and jump about with them, encouraging them to smile and walk tall. This ridiculous game may serve as the starting point for your child's knowledge of what it is like to really feel good about themselves. If they can master this game, they will learn to project feelings of well-being and confidence, even when they do not feel like doing so. Additionally, we have found that some of the youngsters who are not confident learn to like the "Feel Good" section of the exercise and gradually begin to participate with enthusiasm.

Scavenger Hunts

This may require some organization. It is a fun activity that can help your child practice a handful of social skills. It requires cooperation and teamwork, as he/she must work with his/her peers to get clues and acquire prizes along the way.

Board Games

Most children love to play board games. Consider making them a part of your family tradition to have a game night one night per week. Board games help your child cultivate more than one social skill at a time while having fun. Taking turns teaches your child patience and cooperation, and to play. He/she must learn to follow directions, so this is a good activity to engage in on a regular basis. To build on your child's patience, start the game with no more than 3–4 players. As you see your child's patience growing, consider adding a couple more people to your game night to further nurture your child's patience skills, particularly in more of a social environment. Great examples of games to cultivate your child's social learning skills are Candyland, Monopoly, Jenga, Go Fish, and UNO (although the last two are not board games).

Staring Contest

We mentioned this game briefly when we discussed the importance of maintaining eye contact when talking or communicating. Engaging your child in a staring contest is a great way to tackle this, especially if you have a shy child. The staring contest allows him/her to focus on a singular goal, helping you develop his/her social skill in eye contact. Try simulating a conversation with him/her during this contest to get your child in the practice of looking you in the eye when he/she is communicating. After the contest, praise your child and offer a reward to encourage repeating the behavior.

Rhythm Games

The most common rhythm game that you can play with your child is musical chairs. Not only it is fun, but it encourages your child to follow directions, wait for his/her turn, and manage his/her emotions if he/she is left without a chair. It is a fun, engaging game that will allow your child to interact with other children and practice acceptable social behavior.

Chapter 34
How to Help Children in Developing Mindfulness to be Prepared for Life

Relocate to the most desirable community you can afford.

Parents can make the best choice for their children when moving to a community with good schools, better career options, and opportunities to interact with peers who value education, hard work, and achievement. You do not need to be wealthy. Moving to a nicer neighborhood is a better investment than tutoring and extracurricular activities such as music lessons.

Be happy and less stressful by making a conscious effort.

Emotions are contagious, and it is essential to recognize this. If you're depressed and stressed, your children will catch those emotions like a cold from you.

They need to learn how to be "grumpy."

Grit can be taught by cultivating something that "grabs their attention initially but that they get comfortable with enough, educated enough that they awake the next day and so on. Please encourage your children to continue practicing after that and see the benefit of their efforts.

Exhibit self-assurance in your thoughts.

Children absorb the language, thinking, and behavior of those closest to them in their immediate environment, which can be detrimental. They should hear something along the lines of "I'll give it a go." In contrast to "I am not very good at this," saying "I am not very good" is far more effective. Showing children how to reframe their negative self-talk by demonstrating how to find a positive in challenging circumstances may also be beneficial.

Concentrate on making an effort and improving.

According to current thought, people who feel they can improve their intellect via effort and challenge are genuinely more intelligent and do better in school, job, and life over time. One strategy to cultivate a growth mindset is to use language that emphasizes effort and progress rather than the outcomes of what they do or how they perform. By associating success with effort, you instill the belief that success is based on something other than their inherent abilities, talents, or intelligence.

Strategy for receiving praise.

Putting out effort is essential for success, but it is not the only factor. When kids become stuck, they should experiment with different tactics and seek advice from others. They need various ways to learn and progress, rather than simply pure effort. It also aids in concentrating language on better and more intelligent ways of improving. Comments such as, "Wasn't it a great idea to tackle the most difficult assignment when you were still fresh?" "(strategy)" and, "You recognized that the first few steps were the most crucial, but you were wrong after that" are examples of descriptive statements that have excellent teaching value for children.

Develop your self-help abilities from a young age.

The triumphs and accomplishments of a youngster contribute to developing their self-esteem. The most vital qualities to develop to gain confidence are fundamental self-help abilities. These qualities serve as the foundation upon which other competencies, such as organizational skills and various social skills, are built.

More time spent in places where they feel confident will help them grow.

Others excel on the athletic field but struggle in the classroom; they may be fearless risk-takers outside but are held back by self-doubt regarding social situations. While it is true that self-confidence is situational, it is also true that it is transferable. That is, when you experience courage in one aspect of your life, it is common for these sentiments to spread to other parts of your life. Confidence has a snowball effect, so encourage your kid to spend more time in areas where they excel to raise their self-esteem and sense of self-worth.

Most significantly, outstanding parents and instructors have a natural ability to instill confidence in their children's hearts. They find methods to communicate to their children that they believe in them and are confident in their children's ability to perform and achieve. They have trust in their ability to cope with life's obstacles and are satisfied in their ability to grow more independent.

Educate children on the importance of overall health.

Adults and children alike need to cultivate healthy habits to succeed. The best way to ensure that your children get enough sleep, eat healthily, and stay active is to set reasonable limits. In other words, don't allow children to stay all day indoors and watch films. Go outside and let them play. Instead of focusing on their appearance or talking about how awful you feel after buying fast food, teach them the health benefits of taking care of themselves. Make healthy dinners together, go for bike rides as a family, or set aside time to write in your thankfulness journals to instill positive habits in your children.

Make a point of instilling confidence in your children.

One of the best ways to instill a sense of self-confidence in your children is to model these traits yourself. By observing their parents, children learn how to respond in various situations. So, keep an eye on your mental toughness and work on areas where you can improve. Here are a few ideas for teaching your children to be mentally tough.

Become a mental strength role model

In order for your child to develop mental strength on their own, you need to teach them how to be mentally strong. Talking to your child about your personal goals is the best way to motivate yourself. Make your personal development and mental strength a priority, and avoid doing the things that mentally strong parents avoid doing.

As a parent, teach your child to overcome their fears.

As a parent, it's your responsibility to help your child overcome their fear of the unknown. For children who are anxious about being alone, taking small steps can help them overcome their dark fears and meet new people in general.

Mental toughness should be taught in schools.

Be on the lookout for ways to help your children develop mental toughness. You can help them develop the mental toughness they'll need to deal with difficult emotions and situations by putting them in various stressful situations. If you want to teach your children to be mentally tough, here are some particular methods you can do so.

Learn a specific trade or trades.

Rather than punishing your children for their mistakes, discipline should be used to educate them on how to do better in the future. Be particular in your punishments to teach certain abilities, such as problem-solving, impulse control, and self-discipline. In the face of temptation, challenging circumstances, and disappointments, these skills will help your youngster learn how to behave effectively.

Teaching Emotional Intelligence.

Relax and allow your youngster to express their feelings without you intervening when they're upset or depressed; instead of relying on you to control their moods, educate children on how to deal with unpleasant feelings independently. Emotionally intelligent children are better able to deal with life's challenges.

Relax and let your child fail.

Let your child fail, So that they don't feel embarrassed or ashamed about making mistakes. When it's safe to do so, discuss how to avoid making the same mistake again in the future.

Encouraging toughness.

Developing a child's mental strength necessitates focusing on their self-esteem, confidence, and independence. With your kids, work together to improve these areas and encourage healthy habits that will help them grow mentally strong.

Encouraging self-awareness.

Put-downs and catastrophic predictions can hurt children's mental health. Teach your child how to reframe their negative thoughts so that they may think more realistically about the situation at hand. Children need to have a positive view, but also realistic.

Build a persona.

A strong moral compass is necessary for children to make healthy decisions. Make a concerted effort to establish values in your child. Establish a regular schedule for reinforcing your core principles through experiential learning. As an illustration, instead of emphasizing winning at all costs, stress the significance of character traits like honesty and compassion.

Do nothing to assuage your child's fears.

When a child is in distress, it can be tempting to rush to their aid, but doing so will reinforce the idea that they are powerless. Allow your child to make mistakes, allow them to get bored, and insist that they take responsibility even if they don't want to. Struggles can help your child developmental strength if you provide encouragement and support.

Make a point of being thankful.

Your child's mental health will benefit greatly if you teach him or her to be grateful for the good things in life. It's important to teach your child to be grateful for all they have, no matter how bad things get. You can help your child's mood and encourage problem-solving by expressing gratitude.

Assume full ownership of your own life.

Accepting personal responsibility is essential to building mental strength. When your child misbehaves or makes a mistake, allow for explanations but not excuses. If your child blames others for their behavior, feelings, or thoughts, correct them.

Chapter 35
Tools Needed for Children to Develop their Self-Esteem

Top Tools to Develop Self-esteem

We have created a series of step-by-step tools to help fulfil your child's essential needs and raise their self-esteem, so they become happier, more cooperative and more responsible. The following is a selection of tools specifically designed to help nurture your child's self-esteem and maximize their chances of developing a growth mindset and higher emotional intelligence.

Tool 1: Limited choices

Offering your children limited choices enables them to make decisions from a young age and develop confidence. Although these choices are generally limited to two, this autonomy gives them the opportunity to express their individual identity and values, which in turn will help reduce power struggles and conflicts, and make them more willing to comply with your requests.

Limited choices works so effectively because it allows you to share control on your terms instead of letting your child take over. It shows them that you are prepared to trust them, helps give them a sense of control over the situation, and shows them that their opinion matters and that their feelings are being heard. Offering choices also allow children to practice making decisions (good and bad) early on, so it's the best preparation for the 'real world'.

How to give limited choices:

Think of two limited choices or options that suit you.

Present these choices before your child has a chance to oppose what you might suggest (i.e. before a power struggle occurs). This is why you should give limited choices as much as possible throughout the day to replace as many order/commands as you can with a Limited Choice (or other alternative tools such as Asking Questions or Positive & Enforceable Statements).

Tool 2: Positive redirection

As parents, we don't always realize how much of our interaction with our children is in the form of negative statements such as "No you can't have ice cream before dinner" or "Stop slamming that door!" In fact, research shows that 80% of parents' interaction with their children is usually negative. Of course, we have to tell our children "No" from time to time, but the problem is that if we say it too often, it starts to lose its effectiveness, and it can negatively affect their self-esteem and confidence in taking on challenges. Psychologists have found that by simply reducing your use of the word "No" and other negative statements and replacing them with more positive alternatives, you can make a significant difference in your child's behavior and motivation.

How to use positive redirection:

If your child is asking for something that you're not willing to give them, begin your answer with a "Yes" regardless of whether you intend to grant the request or not. This allows you to redirect their request. For example:

As an answer to: "Can I have an ice-cream?" try "Yes sure, you can have an ice-cream after dinner" -instead of "No, you can't have an ice-cream, dinner is in half an hour."

As an answer to "I want this toy" use "Yes, you can put this on your birthday list" -rather than "There's no way I'm buying you this now!"

If your child is doing something that you want them to stop doing, use a positive command (called a "start command") expressed firmly and try to do it without raising your voice. If possible, suggest an alternative activity or an alternative way of doing things.

"Please speak quietly" instead of "Stop yelling!"

"Gently pet the dog" instead of "Stop hurting the dog."

Tool 3: Empathy and validation

Empathy and validation are both essential in helping children learn to trust their feelings and developing emotional intelligence (EQ). Listening is the basis of empathy, and children feel validated and more understood when they feel listened to without judgment and aren't immediately given well-meaning advice.

Strong emotions can be scary for a child experiencing them for the first time, so rather than trying to deny them their feelings, it's much better to use it as an opportunity to connect with them instead. In other words, when we refrain from passing judgment and giving advice, children know that we have no agenda beyond being there for them. And when children trust their feelings, it has a positive impact upon their confidence and self-esteem because they aren't afraid of experiencing strong emotions and trust themselves not to become overwhelmed by them.

How to give empathy and validation:

Connect with them: the best way is to appeal first to the right side of their brain and help engage them into a more receptive state of mind. Use a gentle tone of voice, get down on their level, and if circumstances allow it, offer them a warm embrace. When it comes to redirecting a child's emotions, a hug is one of the most powerful methods available. Studies have shown that hugging someone promotes the creation of dopamine and oxytocin in the brain, which both aid to relieve tension while also promoting a sense of enjoyment and relaxation.

Don't deny your child his or her feelings or try to save them from it. Don't tell your child: "It's going to be okay" or "Come on, it's not that bad!" or "Calm down".

Do not immediately ask your child, "Why are you crying?" even if you have no idea why they are in such emotional distress. Much of the time children find it hard to answer this question, and asking it doesn't help them process their emotions. If you really need to because your child is not sharing the reason, you can ask this after following the steps below.

Meet them "where they are" by acknowledging their feelings and help name them. Your child may not be able to understand, acknowledge, or explain the emotion they are experiencing; therefore, you can help them by reading the signs of an emotional state in their behavior and body language (just as one might look for telltale signs of tiredness). This includes "negative" emotions such as anger or sadness. Helping them put a name to their emotions enables them to own this feeling, and therefore control it. Words are not only powerful, but they also serve to normalize things, transforming them from an unknown, amorphous mass into something that can be understood and dealt with more effectively.

When your child has hurt themselves: "Oh, this must hurt!" or "You seem in a lot of pain, the fall must have been harder than it looked?"

When your child is getting very angry with their sibling: "I can see that this situation is upsetting you."

Help your child redirect their emotions (only once you have done the above). When your children are younger, an effective way to do this is to put them in "thinking mode".

When your child has hurt themselves: "Do you need help getting up or can you do it by yourself?" or "Does this hurt a lot, average or just a bit?" or "Would a hug make you feel better?"

In most other situations, you can ask your child, "Is there something that I can do to help?"

Tool 4: Problem Solving

As parents, we often skip straight to offering solutions to our children when they present us with a problem or to implement consequences or punishment when they misbehave, without giving them the opportunity to solve their own issues or try to understand the reasons for their behavior. In doing so, we are underestimating their ability to solve their own problems and not giving them an actual chance to participate in finding solutions to these problems for themselves.

The problem solving tool empowers your children to find solutions to their own problems, rather than focusing on consequences and punishment (which can have detrimental effects on motivation). It's a great way of teaching your child to think for themselves and encourages them to be responsible for their actual own actions, which makes it far more effective than any other form of discipline and a great boost to confidence and self-esteem.

How to use problem solving:

This tool can be used in two different ways:

If they say, "No thank you", say "Okay, but if you change your mind, I'm always here to listen."

If they say, "Yes please", give them some different options of possible solutions. Offer them at least two solutions.

Empowerment: after you explain each solution, encourage your child to evaluate it by asking, "How would that work for you?". If you can't actually come up with any ideas straight away, simply say to your child, "Let me have a think about it and check how other kids have dealt with this problem and I'll get back to you."

Show interest, but avoid interfering: once your child has decided on which solution they think would be the most appropriate course of action (either one you have suggested or one they have come up with themselves), all you need to say is, "Let me know how it actually all works out - good luck!"

When you have a problem that you want to discuss with your child: perhaps you would like your child to improve a certain aspect of their behavior and you want to involve your child in finding solutions to this issue.

Initiate a problem-solving session: the most effective way is by doing something that your child enjoys or, alternatively, you can incorporate this session into a family meeting. Identify exactly what the issue is without blaming your child for the behavior, while explaining why this doesn't work for you.

Ask your child questions that show that you're in it together: "What could WE do about this?"

Work together with your child to generate what possible solutions there may be to the problem in question. Talk about what you could both do differently next time the problem presents itself.

Listen to their suggestions carefully, asking them, "And how do you think that would work for you?"

Have a brainstorming session: decide on what you each think are the best solutions and then brainstorm together about how you could implement them.

Ask your child how they would prefer to be reminded should they break your agreement.

Tool 5: Family meetings

Holding regular family meetings is key to building and maintaining a strong connection with your children and building their confidence and self-esteem. It provides the perfect forum in which to give encouragement and praise and discuss challenges and how to overcome them. It's also a way of making sure that all family members feel a sense of belonging and responsibility towards one another, while providing an invaluable opportunity for each person to have their thoughts heard and their feelings acknowledged. This in itself is incredibly powerful as it helps to create a feeling of family unity and togetherness and a stronger sense of confidence in the strength of the family bond.

How to hold family meetings:

Schedule (ideally) one family meeting every week.

Although it may sound formal, to make the meeting run more smoothly, we recommend electing two family members to act as Chairperson and Secretary (who will be responsible for taking notes of the meeting).

Open the meeting with compliments and gratitudes. Each person should take a turn addressing every family member to express a gratitude or give a compliment. This is a great opportunity to use your new skills to praise the effort and progress that your children have made over the week(s). It also significantly boosts their confidence as they feel that they are noticed and acknowledged.

Ask every family member to share a moment that they have been proud of since the last meeting. Another great confidence booster!

Go through the agenda, which may include one or more of the following:

Individual issues: each family member has the opportunity to raise their need or identify a problem they may be experiencing.

Hold a problem solving session to deal with any individual issues.

Decide on a task/chore system: allocate tasks and household duties.

Plan activities and family fun days.

Play a game or have a sing-song.

It may actually sound a bit cheesy, but it adds to the sense of bonding to end the meeting with a family hug!

Conclusion

As we've seen, self-esteem and confidence are keys to success, and there are many ways we can help to develop these traits in our children. Being aware of the impact that our words and actions have upon our children's personal development and their sense of self is an essential part of the process. We also need to be aware of the most common parenting mistakes so we can avoid making them and prevent our children from adopting a fixed mindset.

Although there is no such thing as a perfect parent, there are steps that each one of us can take to become more effective in our parenting and equip our children with all the tools they need to thrive. Of course, there will be difficulties and challenges along the way, but never despair. There are countless examples of children who appear to dislike school and other forms of learning who are labeled as lazy and not capable by their teachers and others, but still go on to achieve great things in life.

We must remember that as parents, one of the most important jobs we have is to show our children that we will always believe in them, no matter what. When we allow our children to make affordable mistakes, and they see that we have faith in their ability to survive hurt, upset and disappointment, they start to develop more faith in themselves. And when we empower our children to believe in themselves, we also empower them to become happy and independent adults. So when spending time with your children, keep the following in mind:

Show children how to celebrate their mistakes by embracing yours to help make them more resilient which will increase their willingness to take on new challenges.

Refrain from rescuing them from difficult experiences and unpleasant emotions: this will help train their "disappointment muscles:, and better prepares them for the realities of adult life.

Help them see that in every difficulty or challenge they face lies an opportunity for learning and growth.

Always focus on the effort and progress your child has made when participating in a task, exam, or activity rather than the outcome as this will help them develop a growth mindset and the art of self-motivation.

Be selective and honest in the praise you give and remember to ask questions to help them self-evaluate (such as "You must be proud of yourself given all the efforts you've put into this") before giving your own judgment and praise.

If you are consistent in the application of the tools in this book, you can maximize the chances that your children will one day - hopefully sooner rather than later - develop a growth mindset, find their passion(s), and become completely responsible for their own success.

Scarlett Steele

www.ingramcontent.com/pod-product-compliance
Lightning Source LLC
Chambersburg PA
CBHW070653120526
44590CB00013BA/941